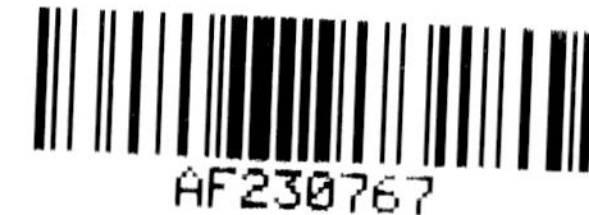
AF230767

Puppy Love

A Delightful Journey of Creativity and Cuteness!

Coloring Book

Crystal Moon

ISBN: 978-0-9888737-4-2

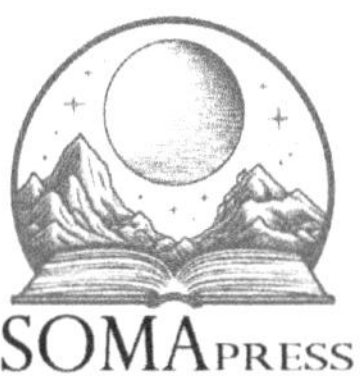

SOMAPRESS

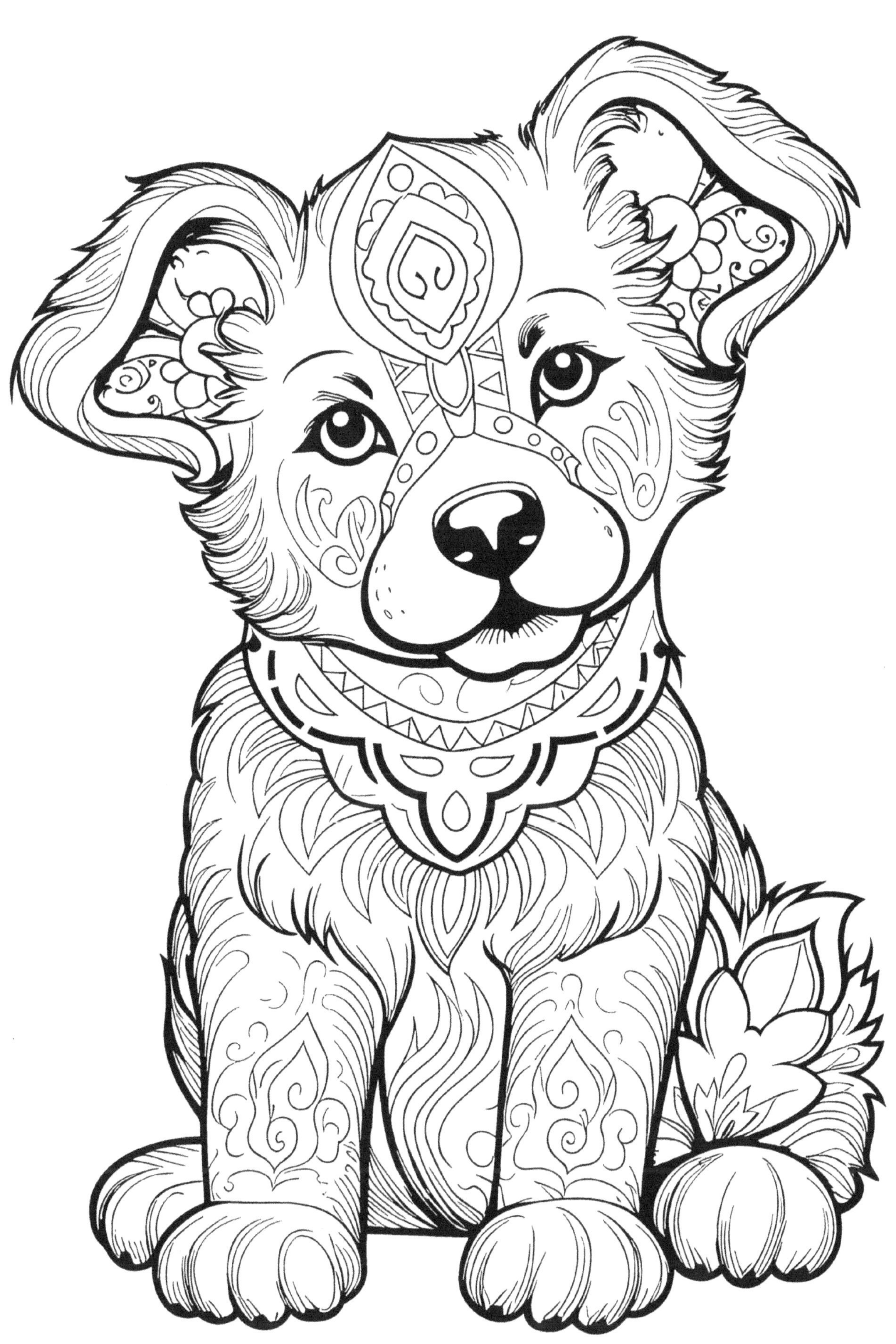

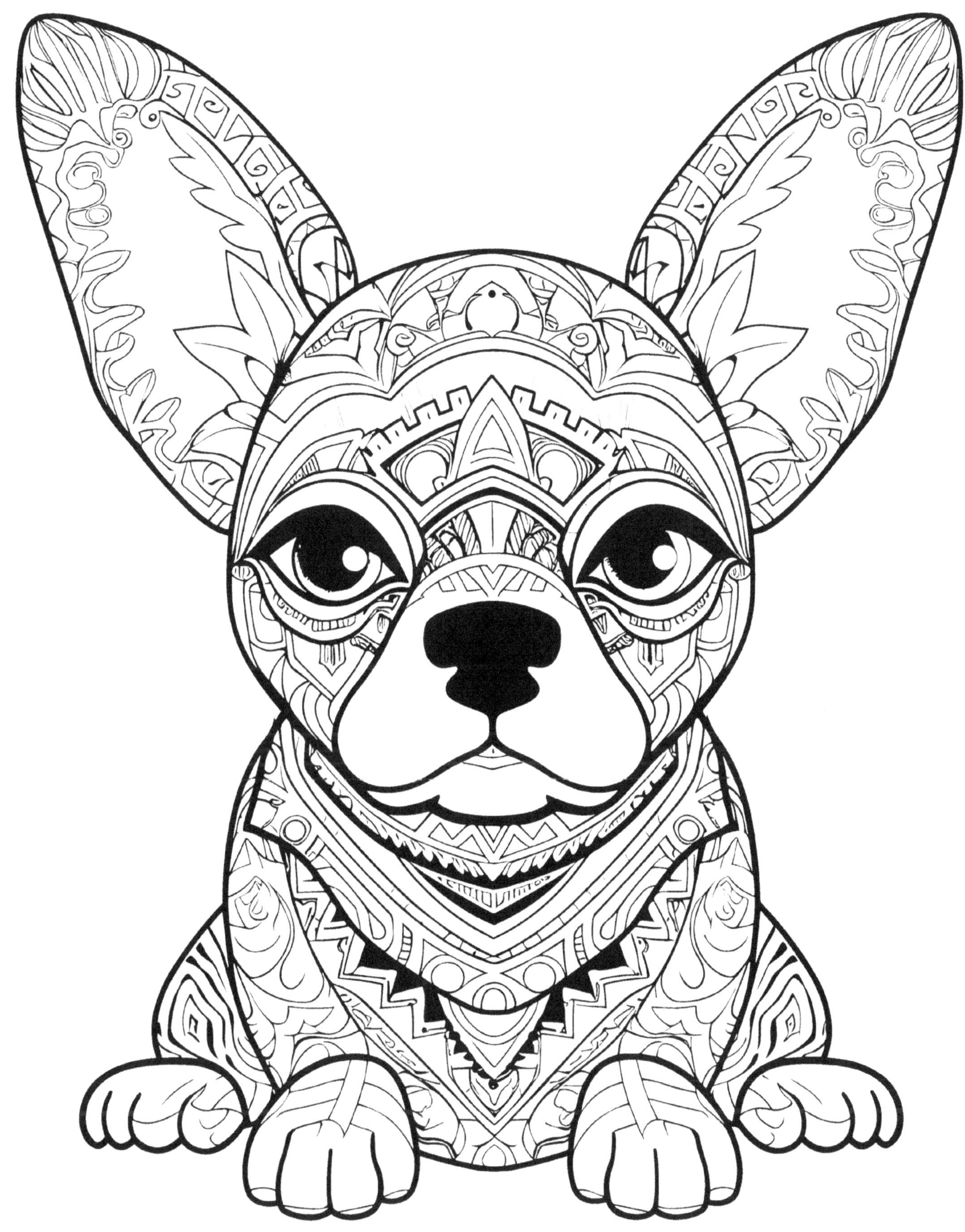

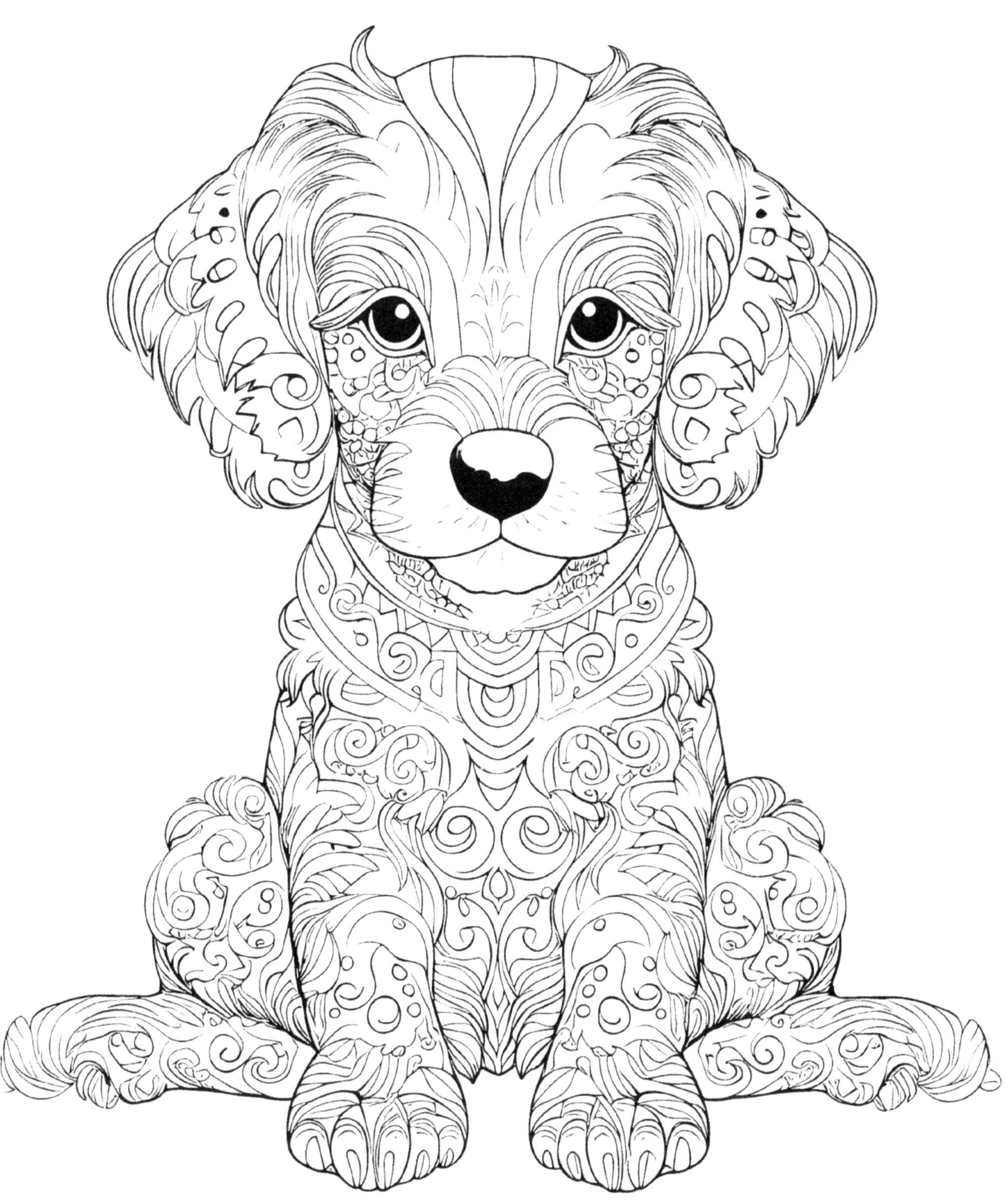

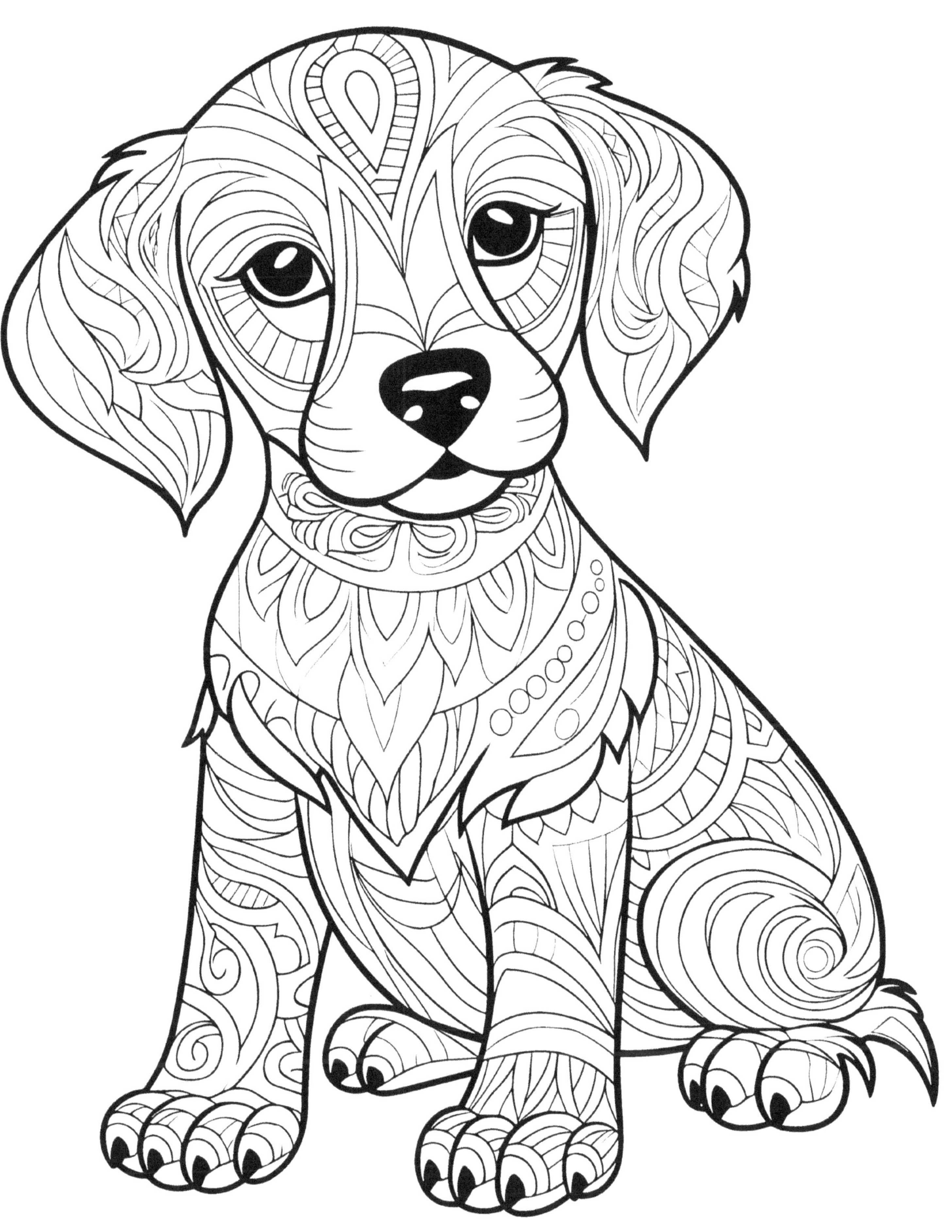

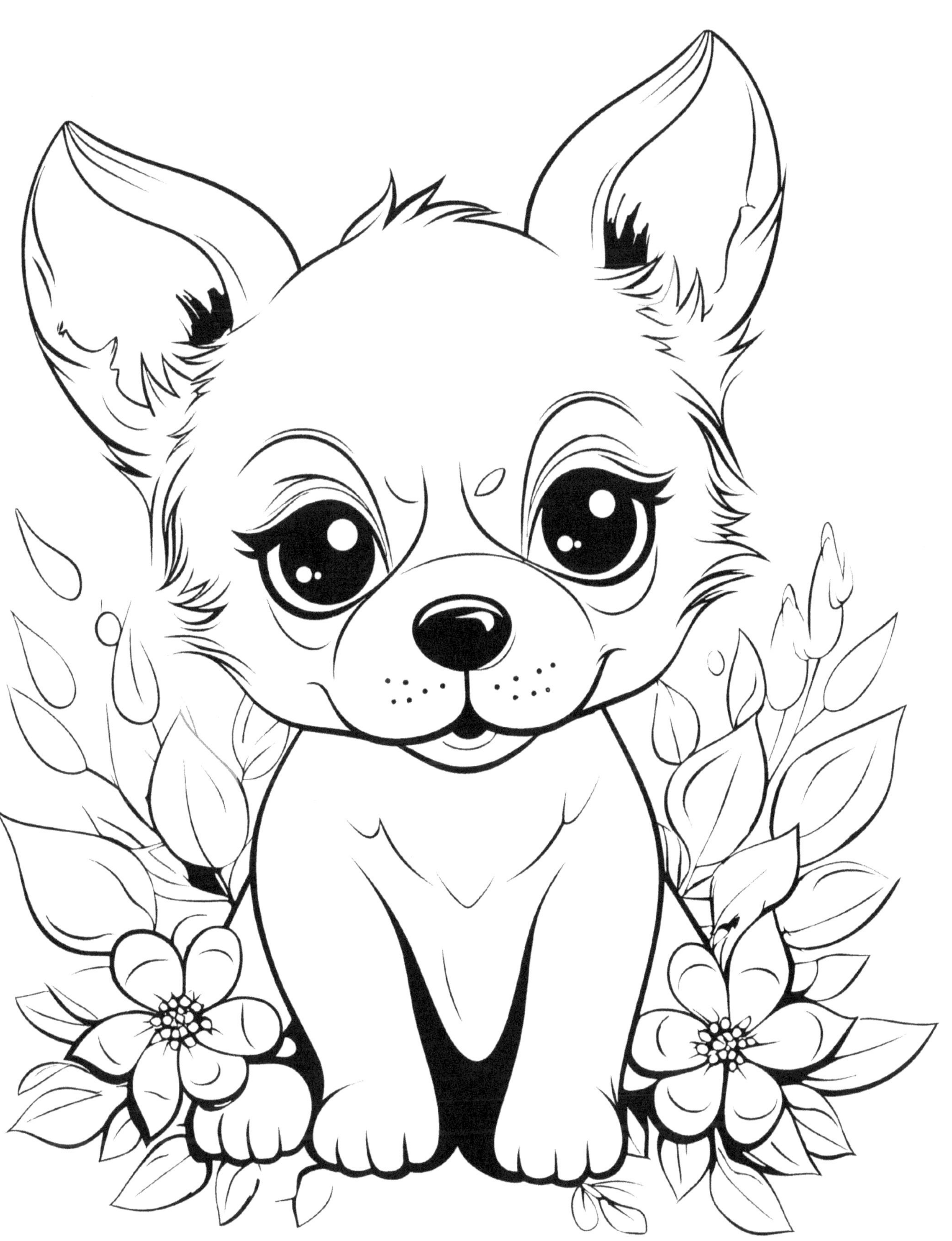

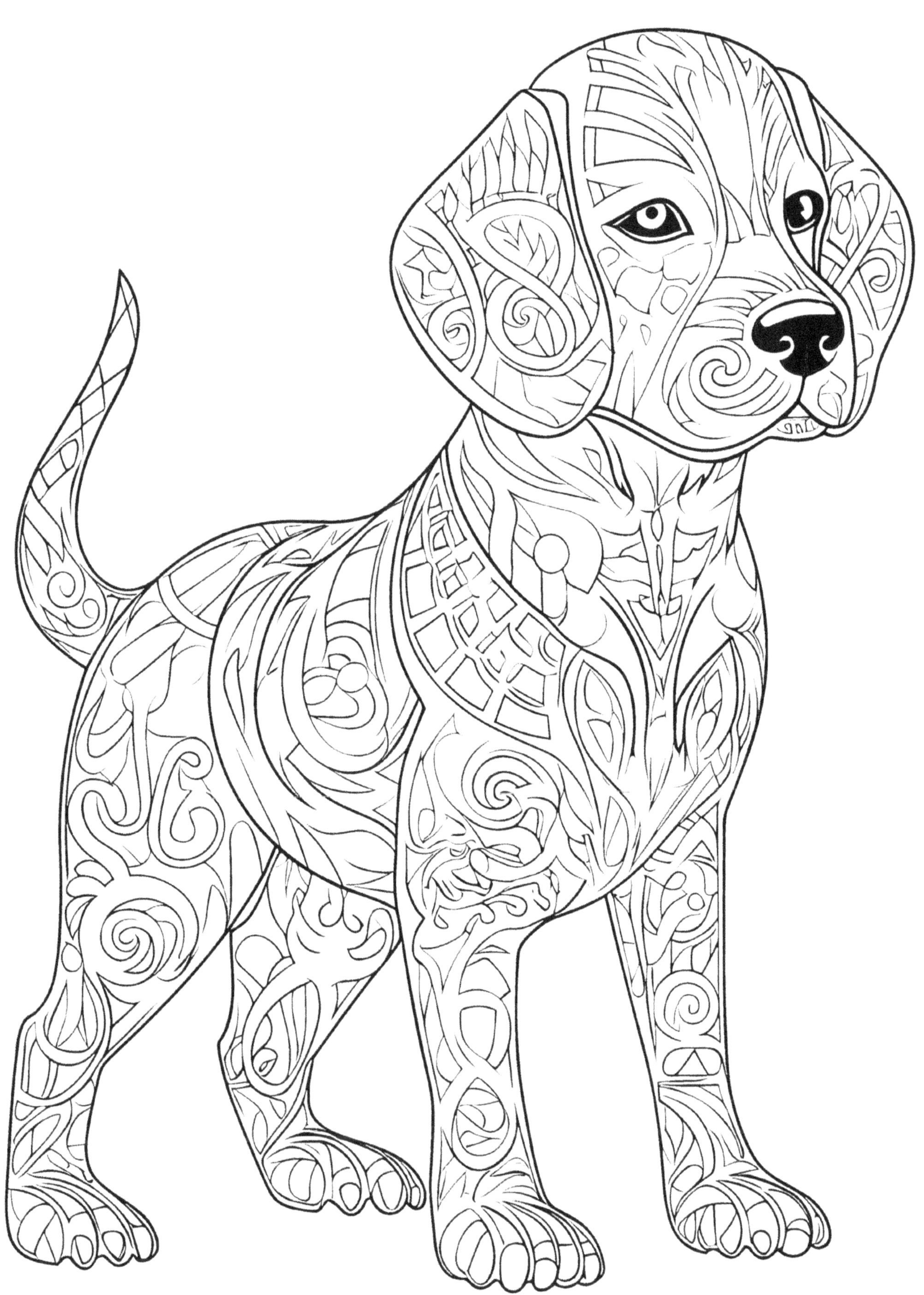

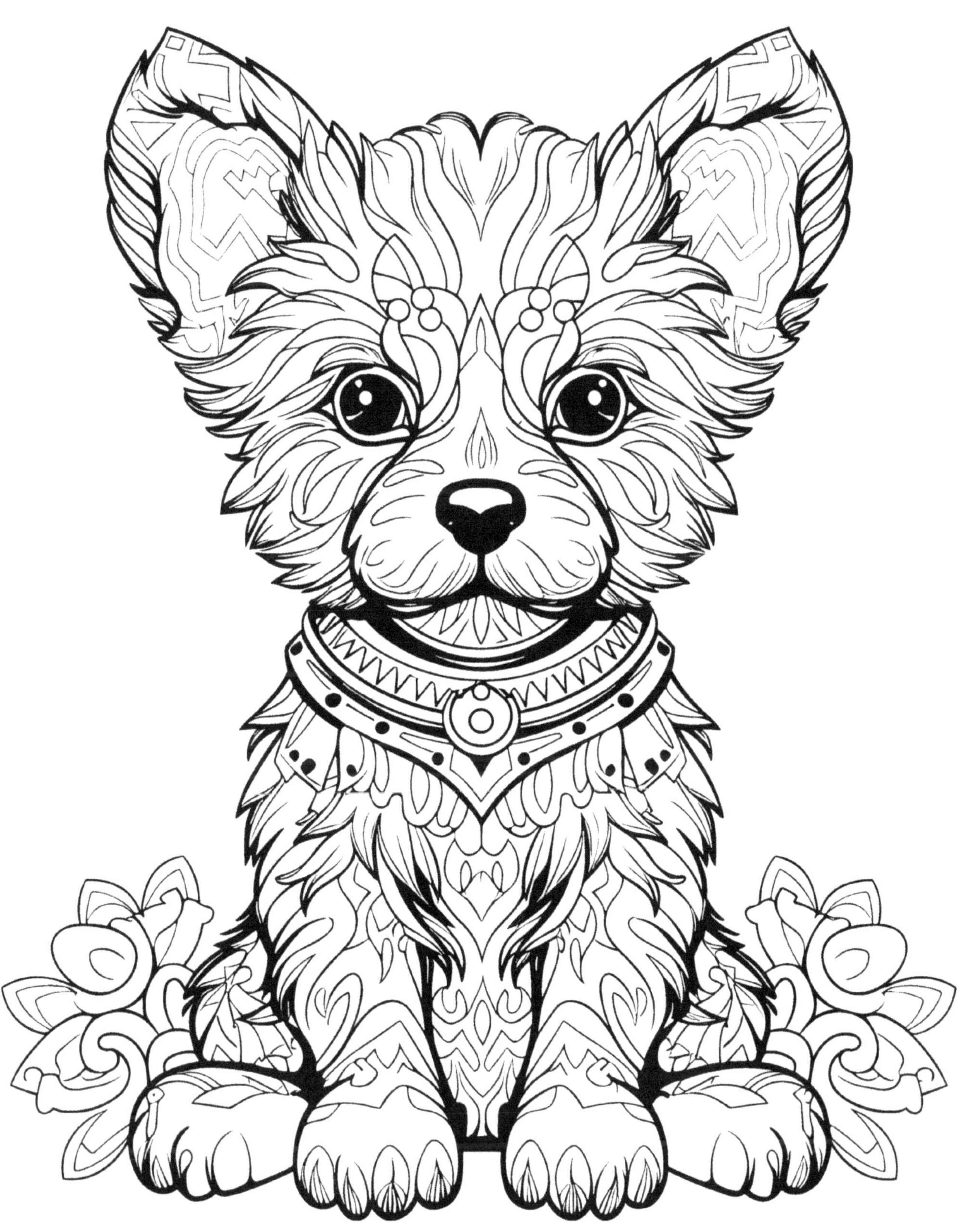

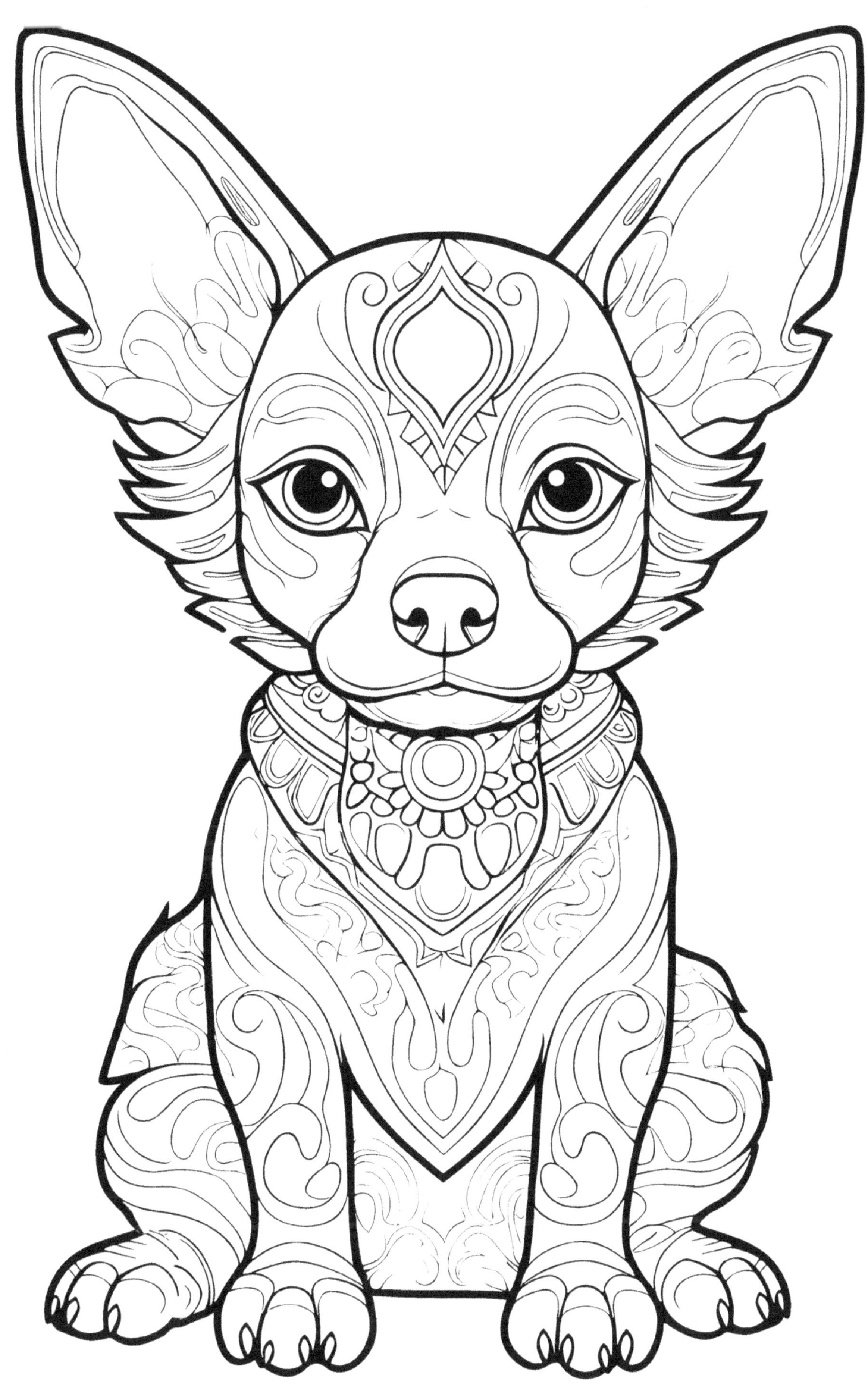

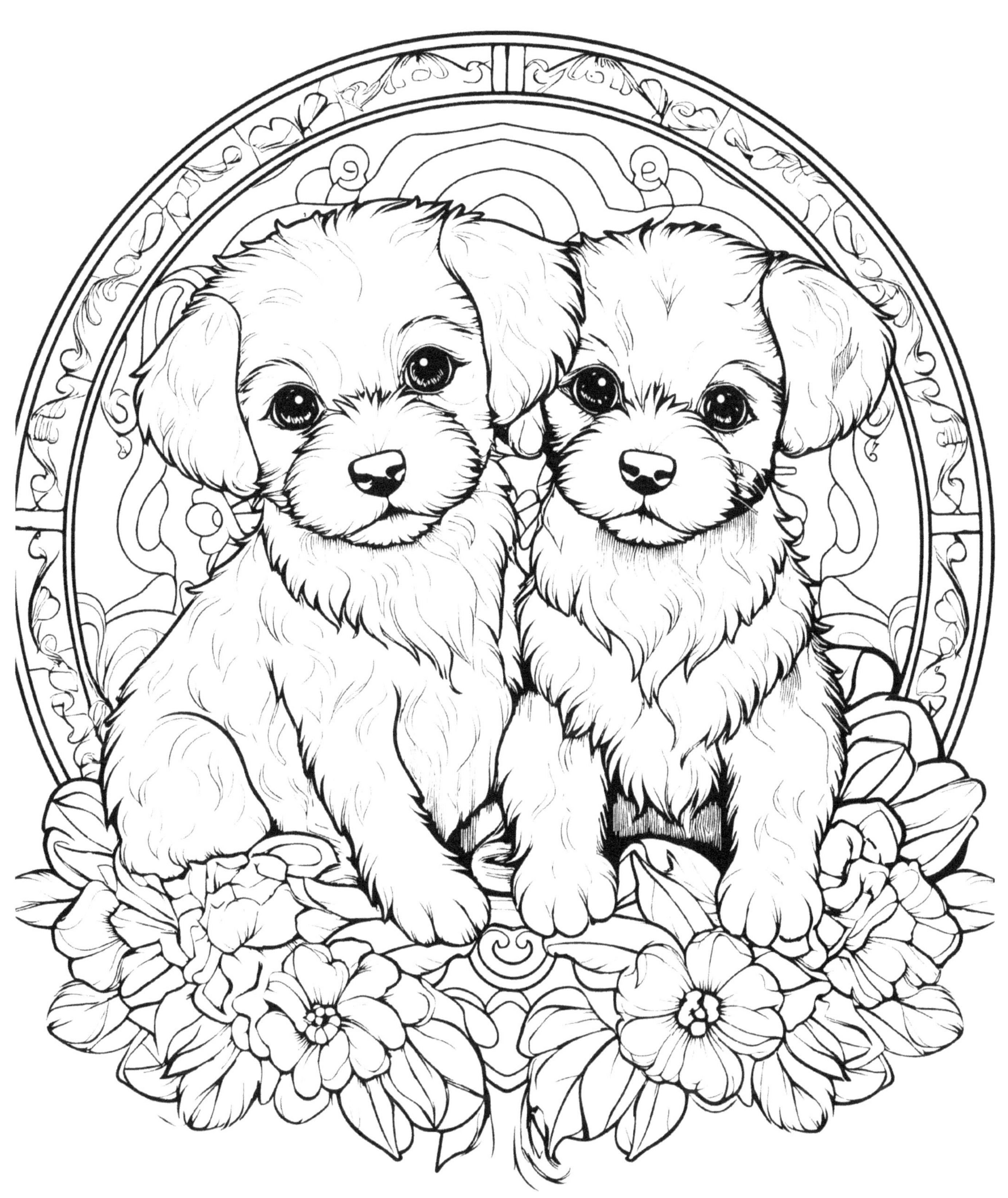

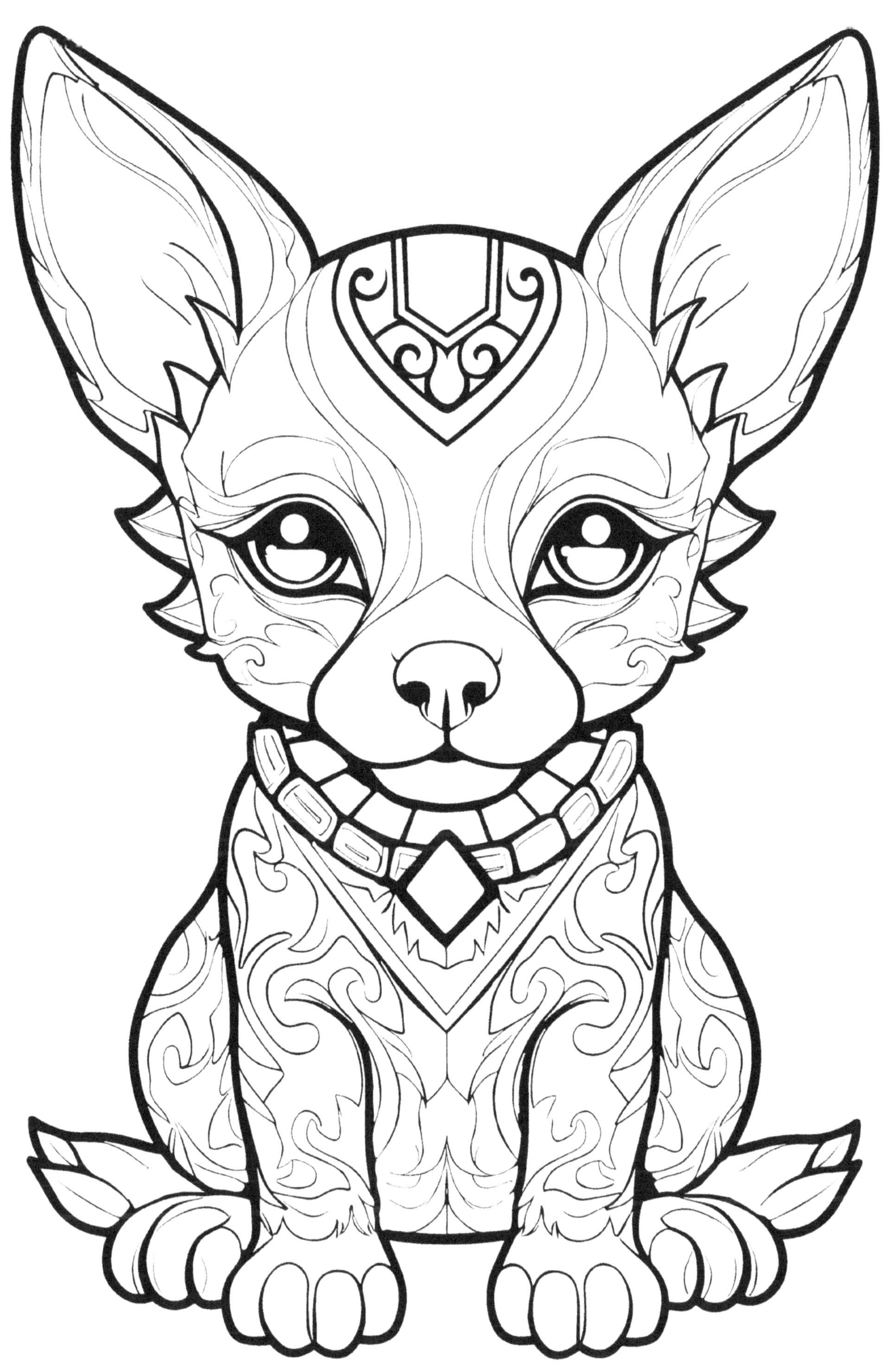

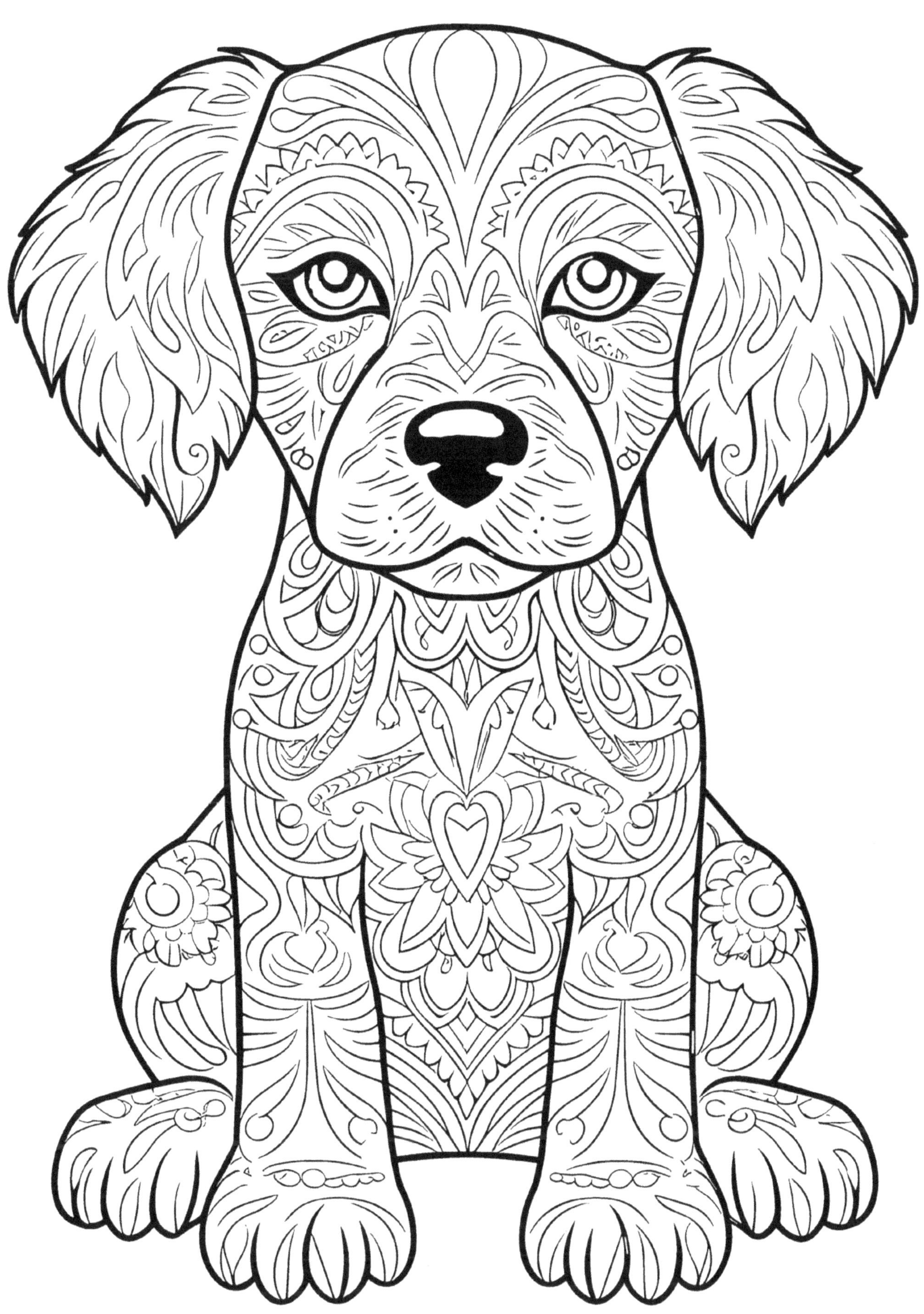

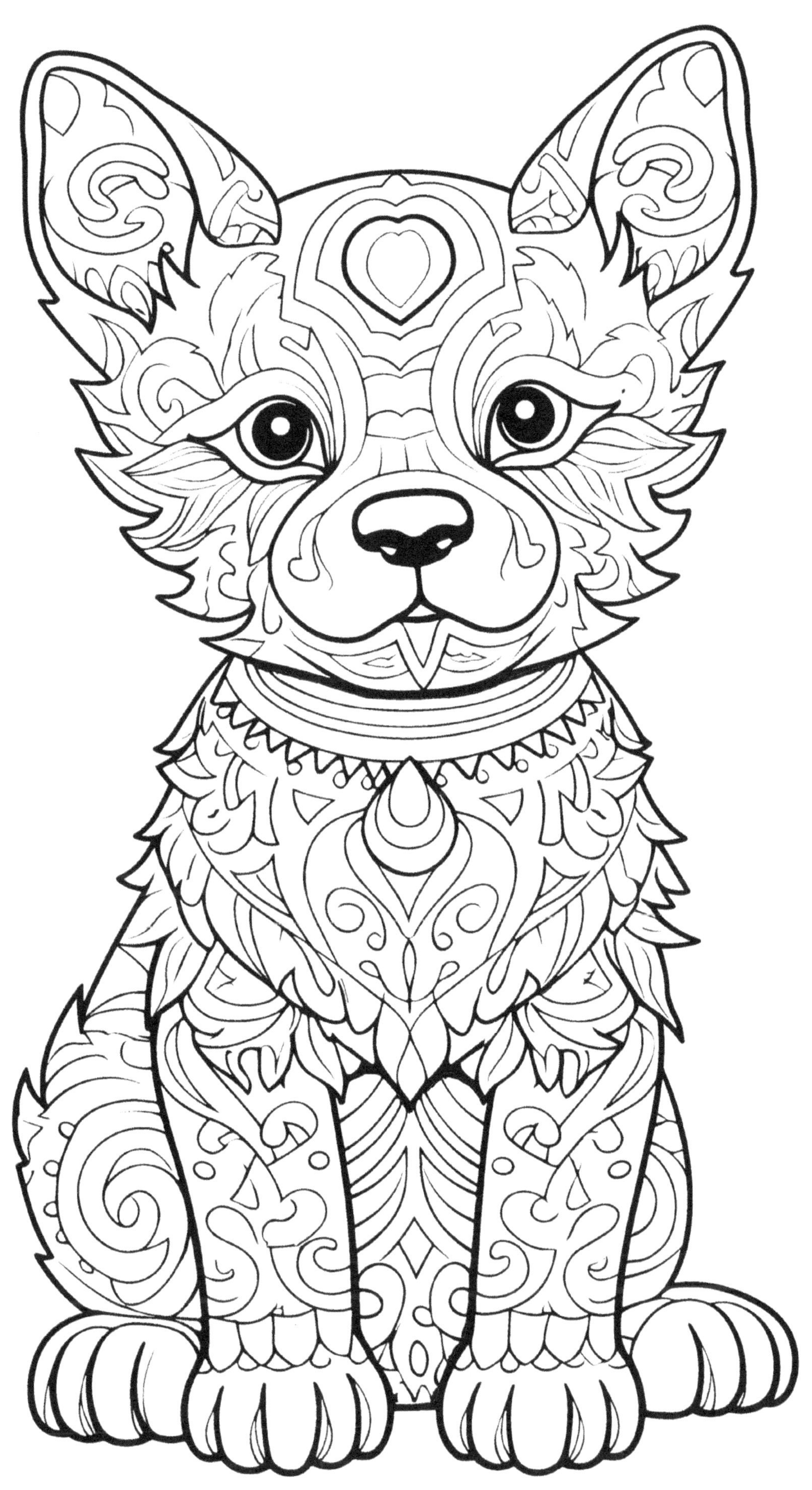

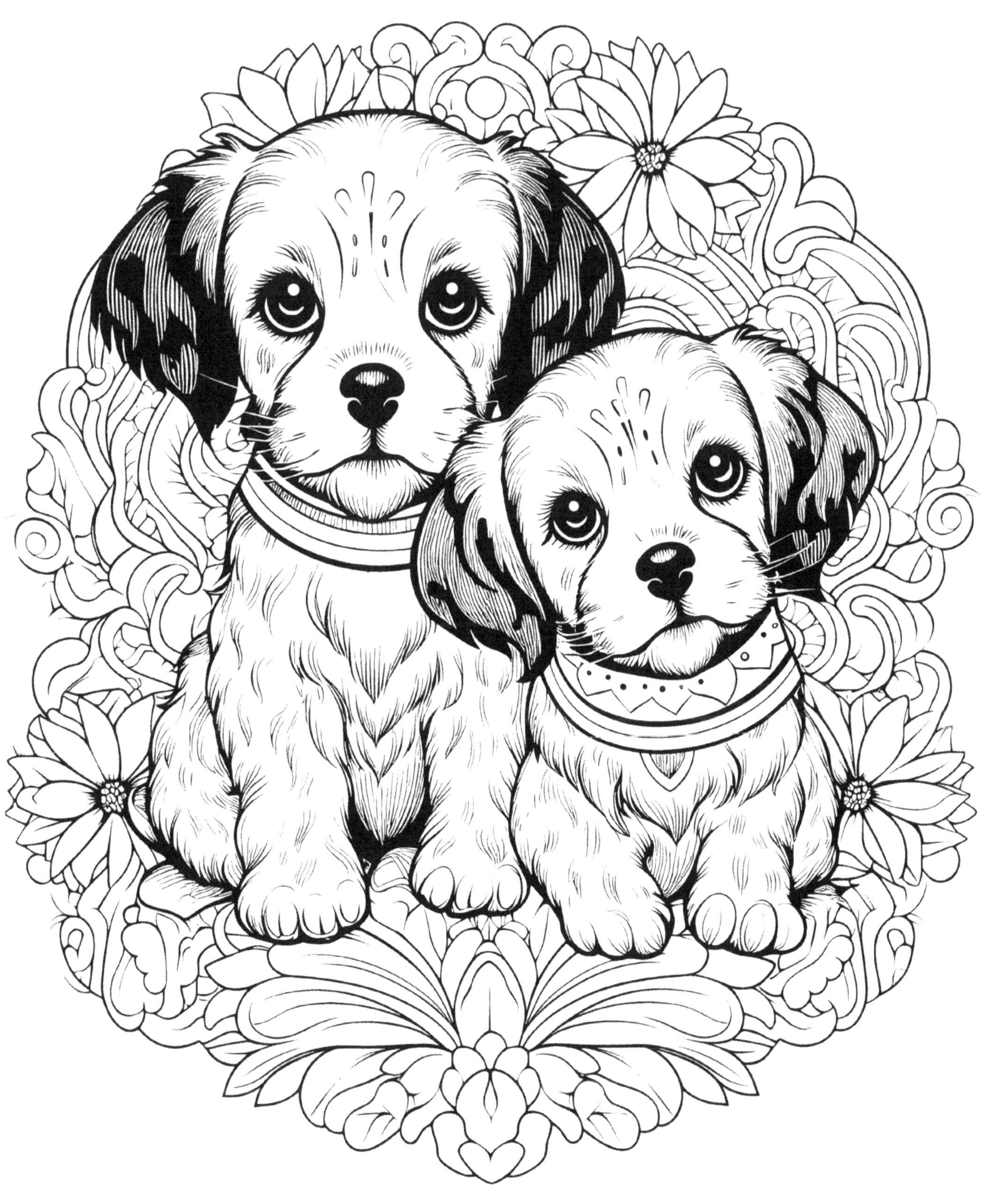

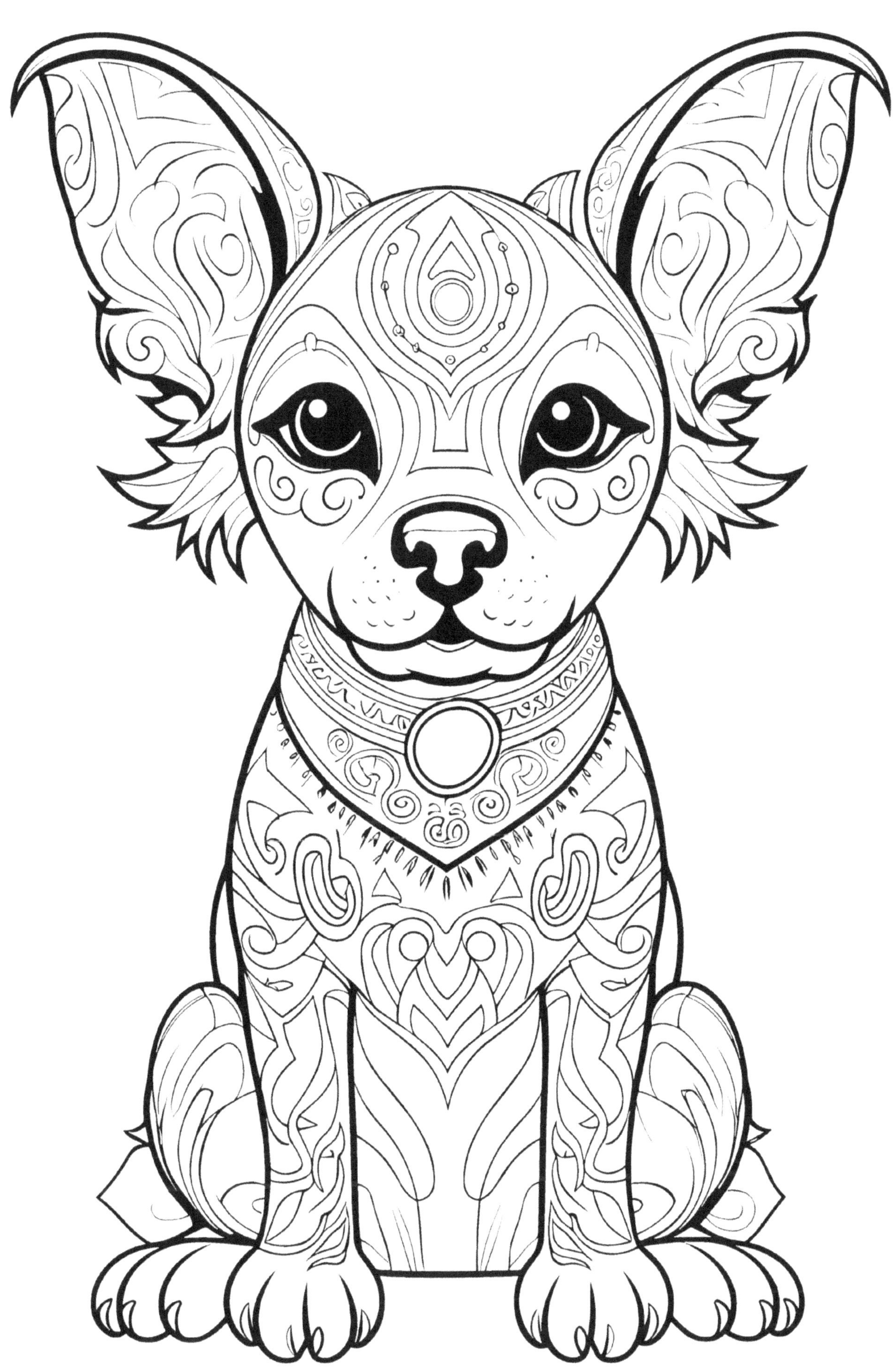

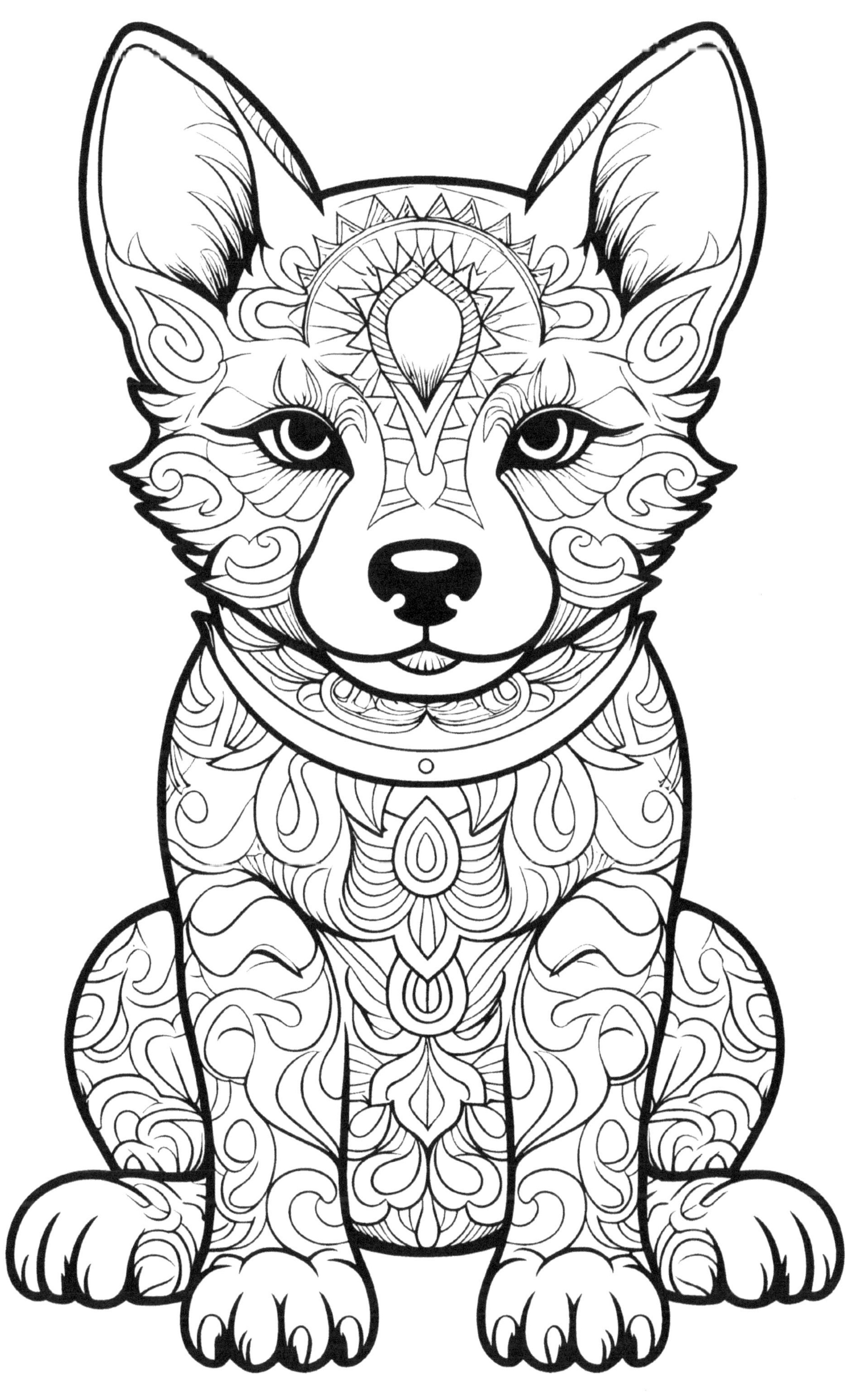

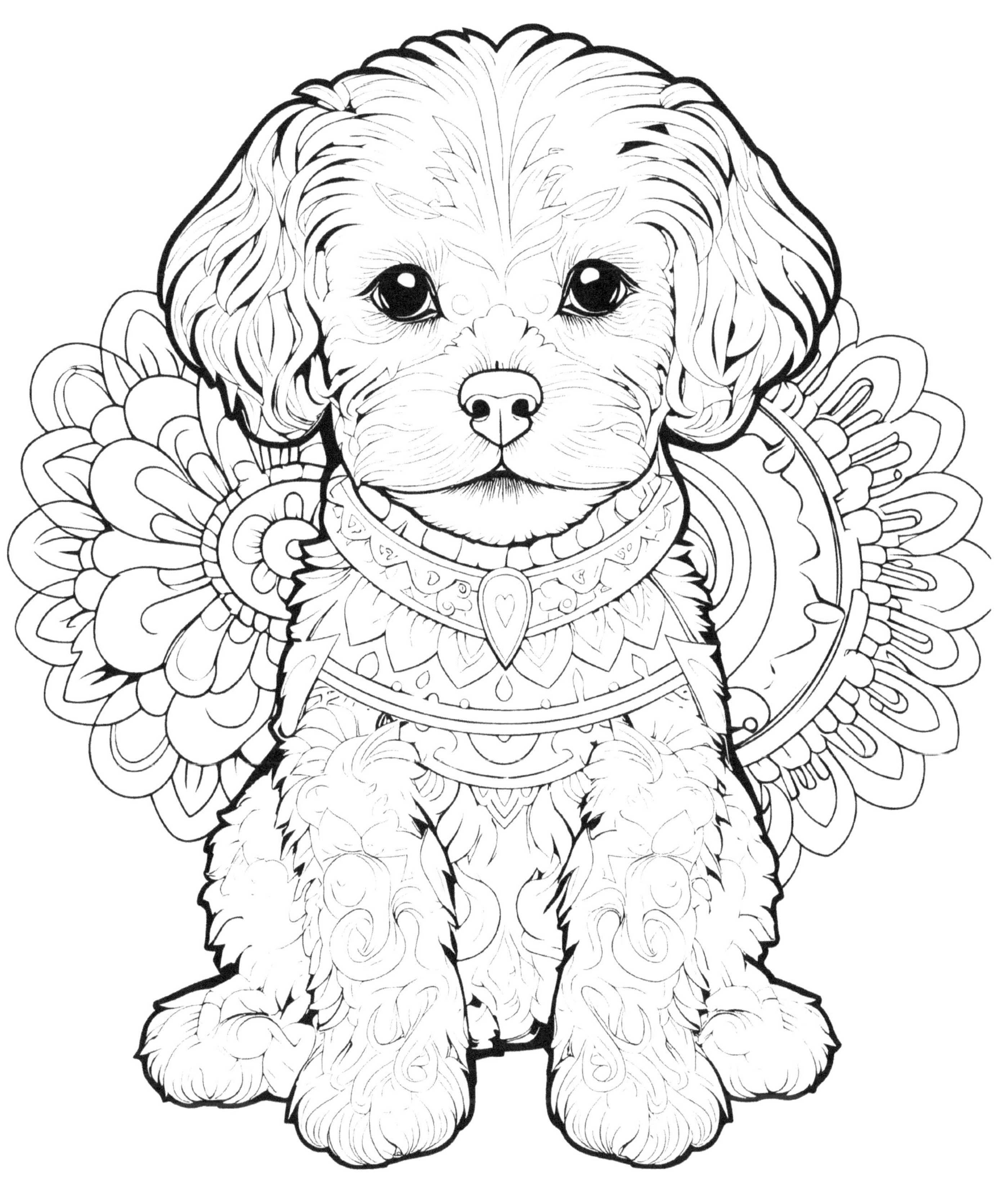

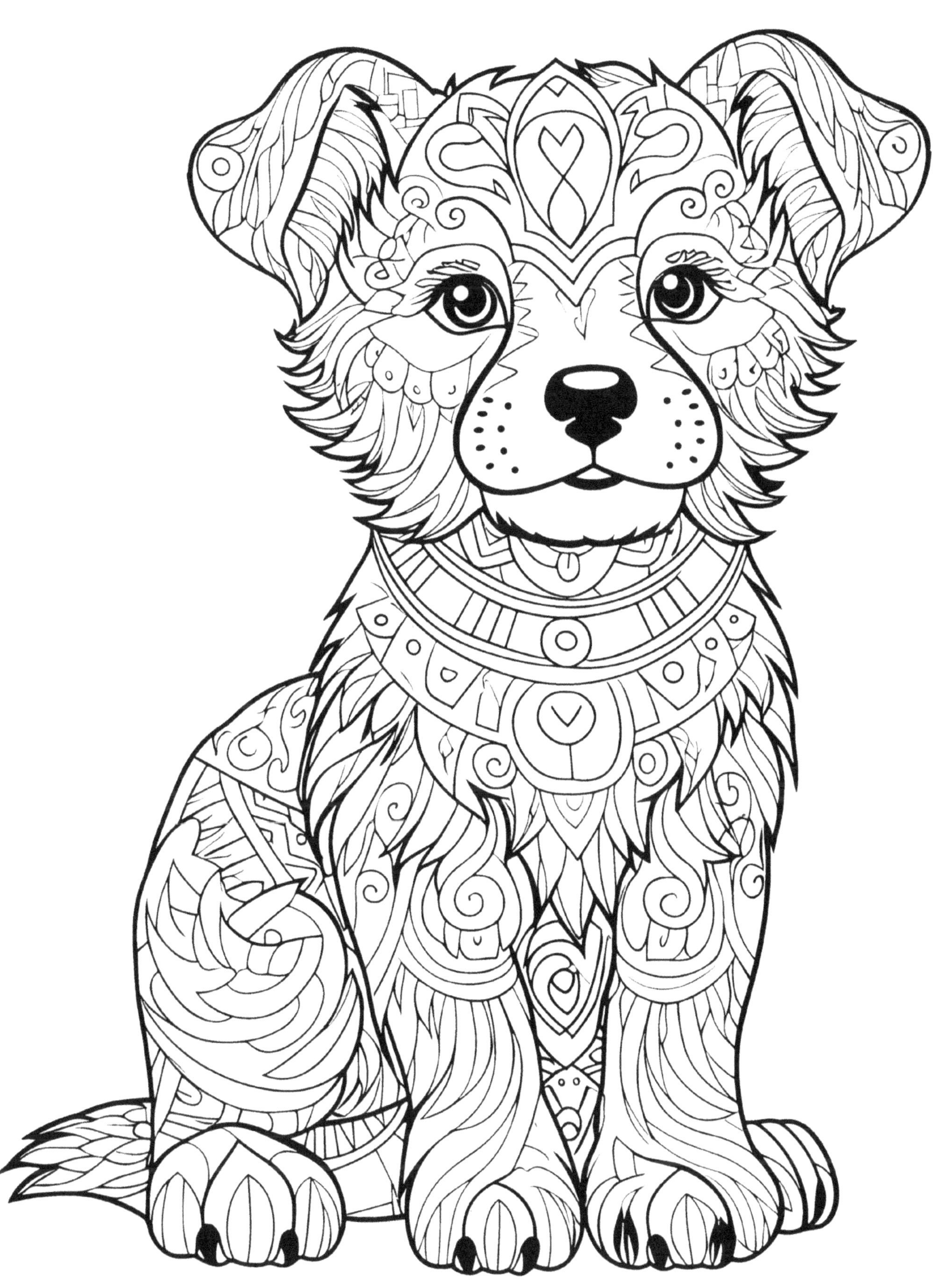

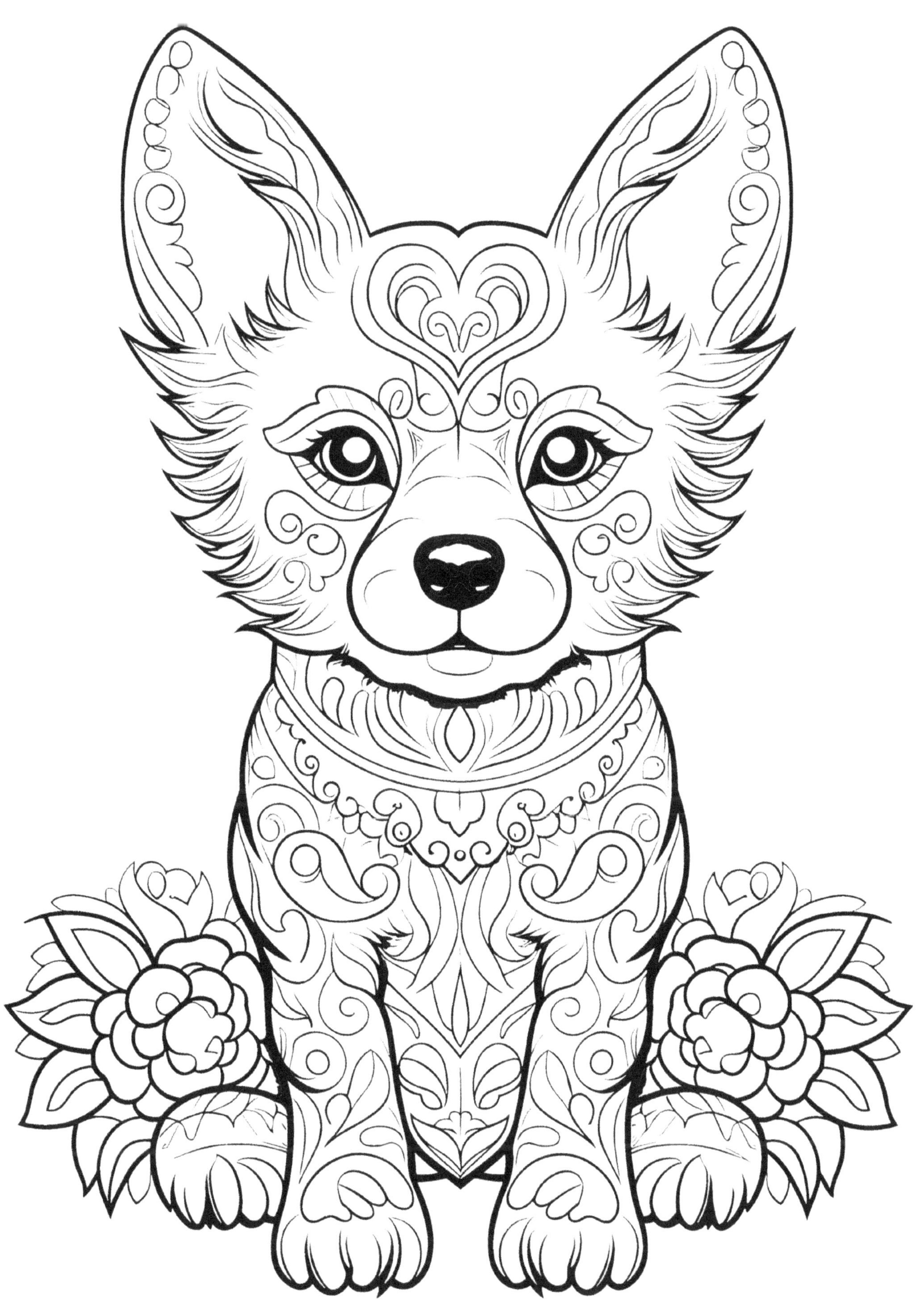

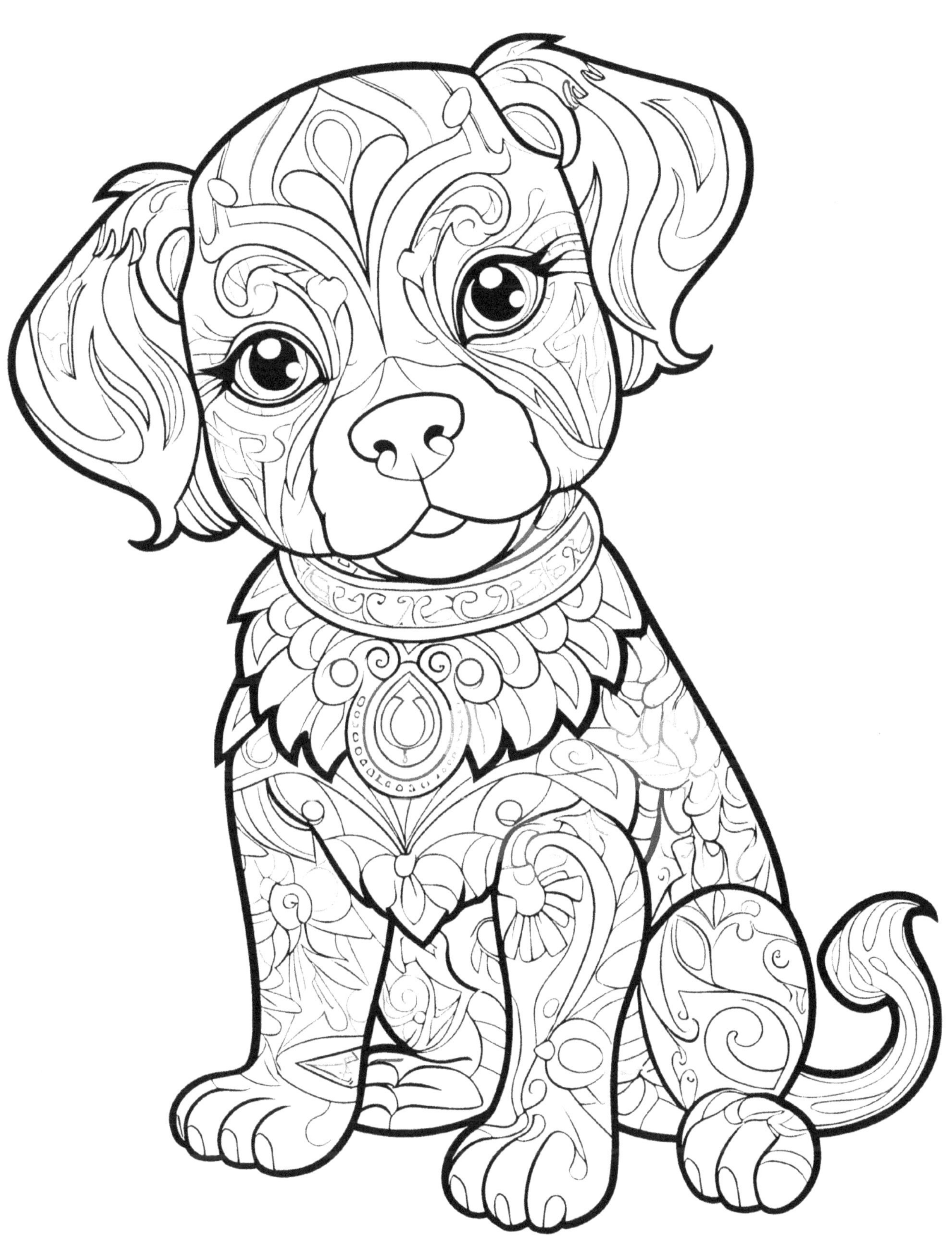

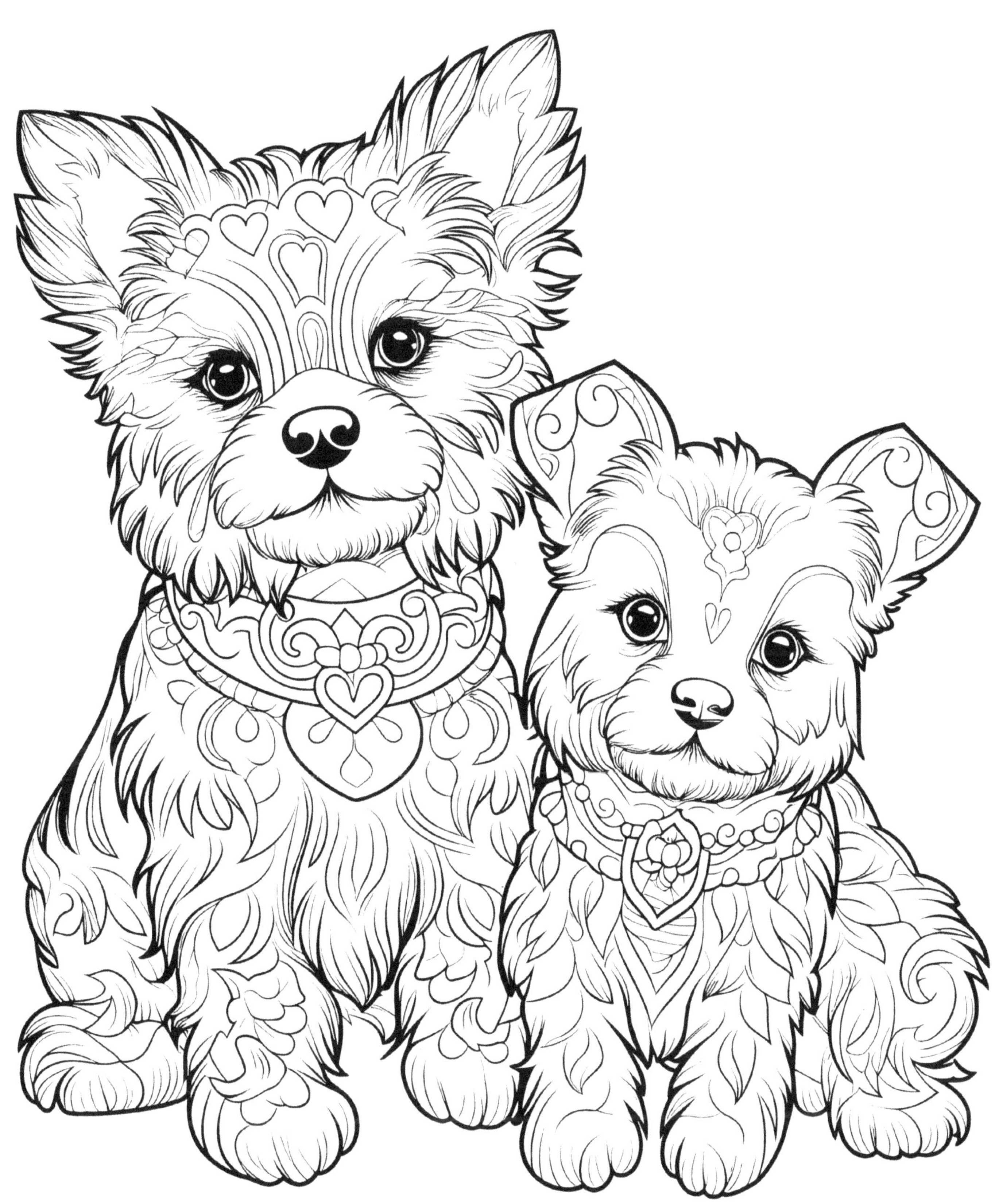

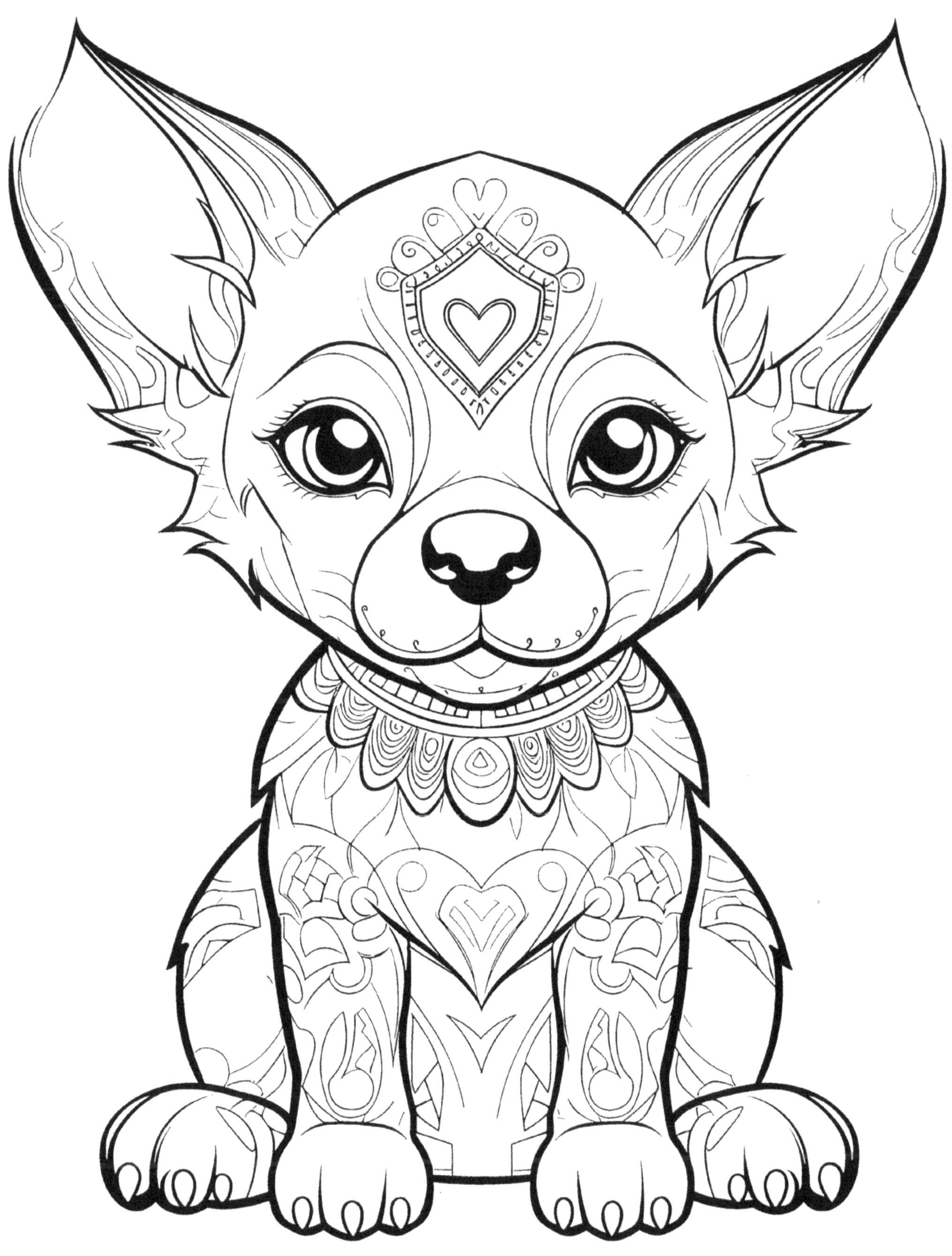

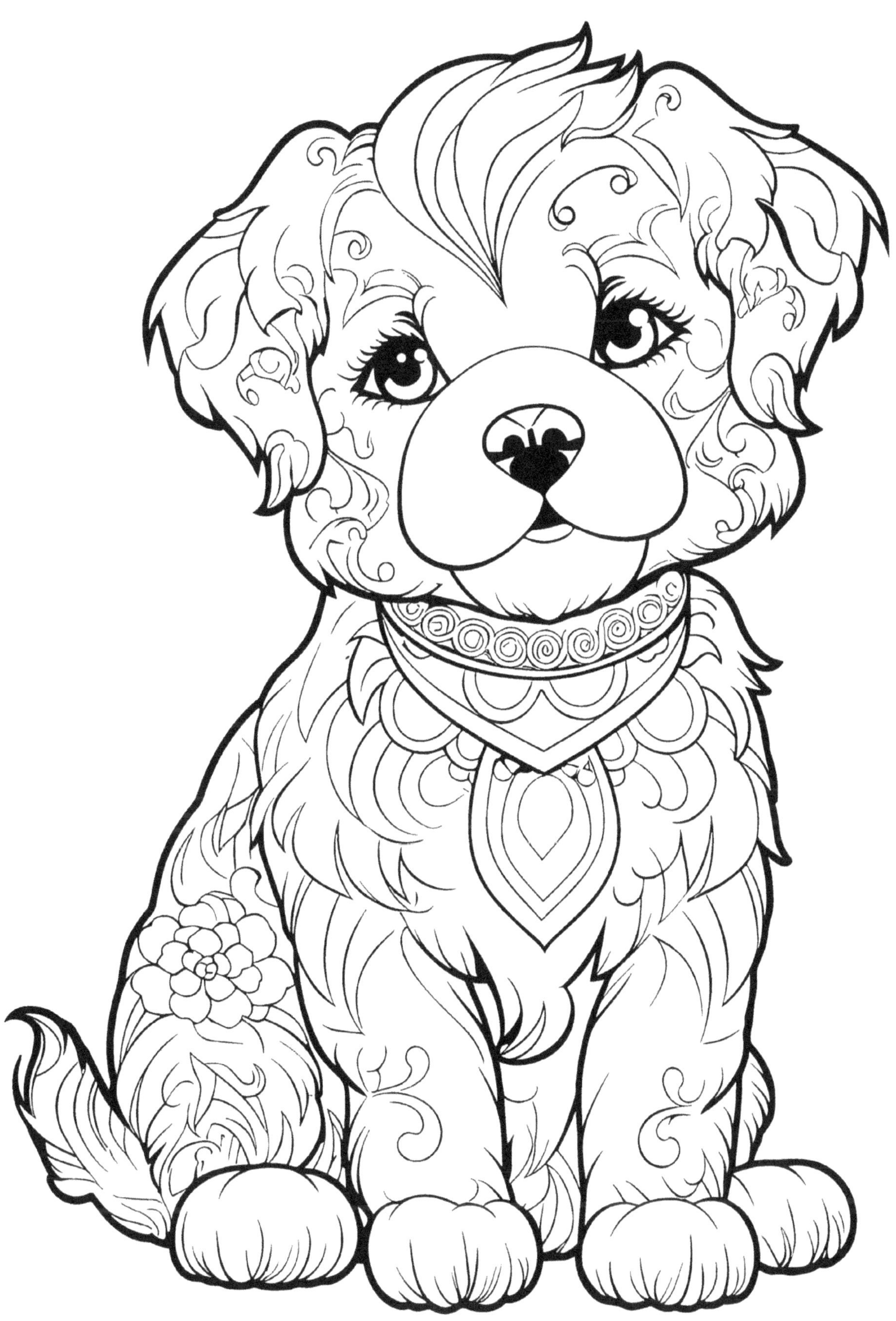

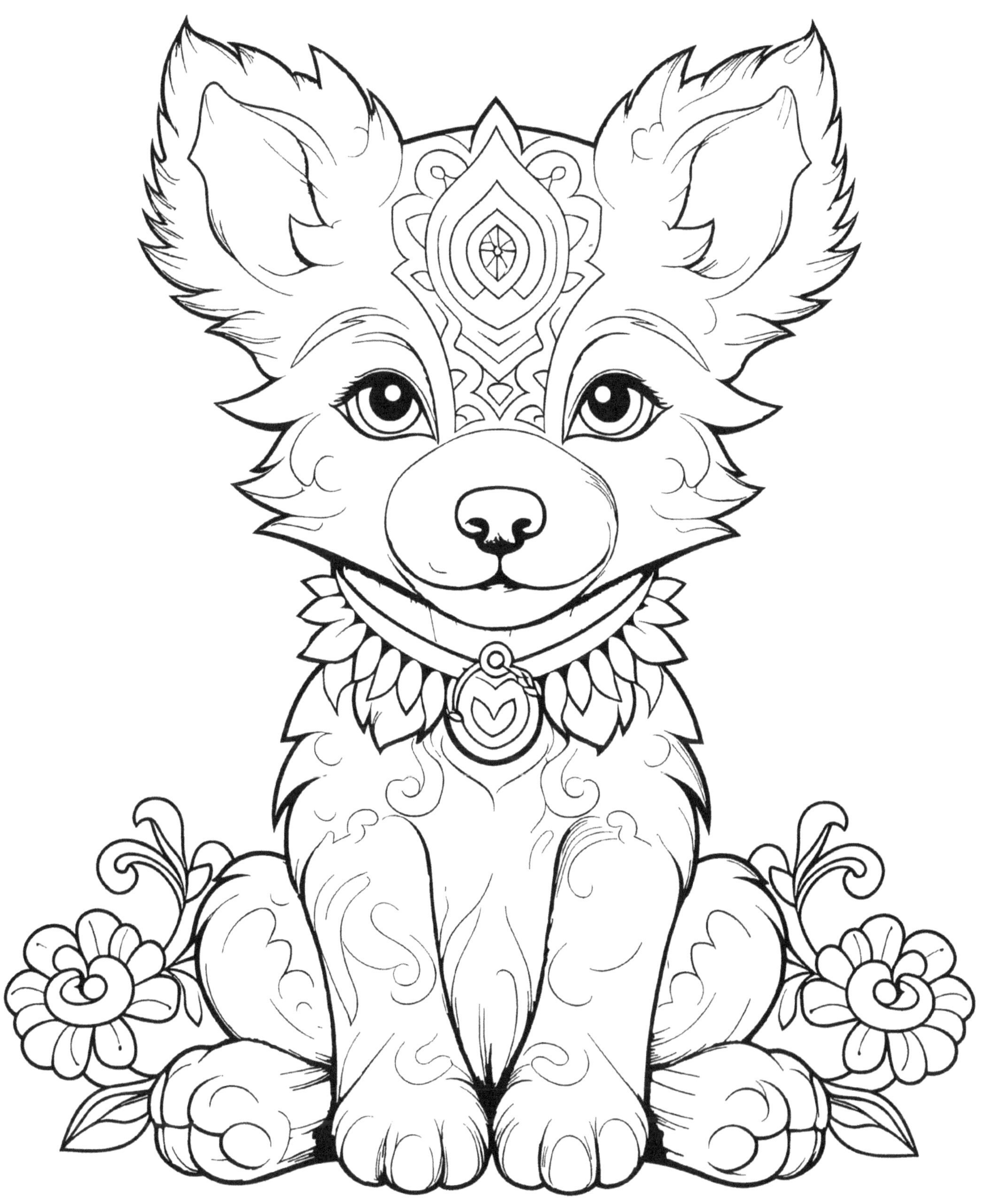

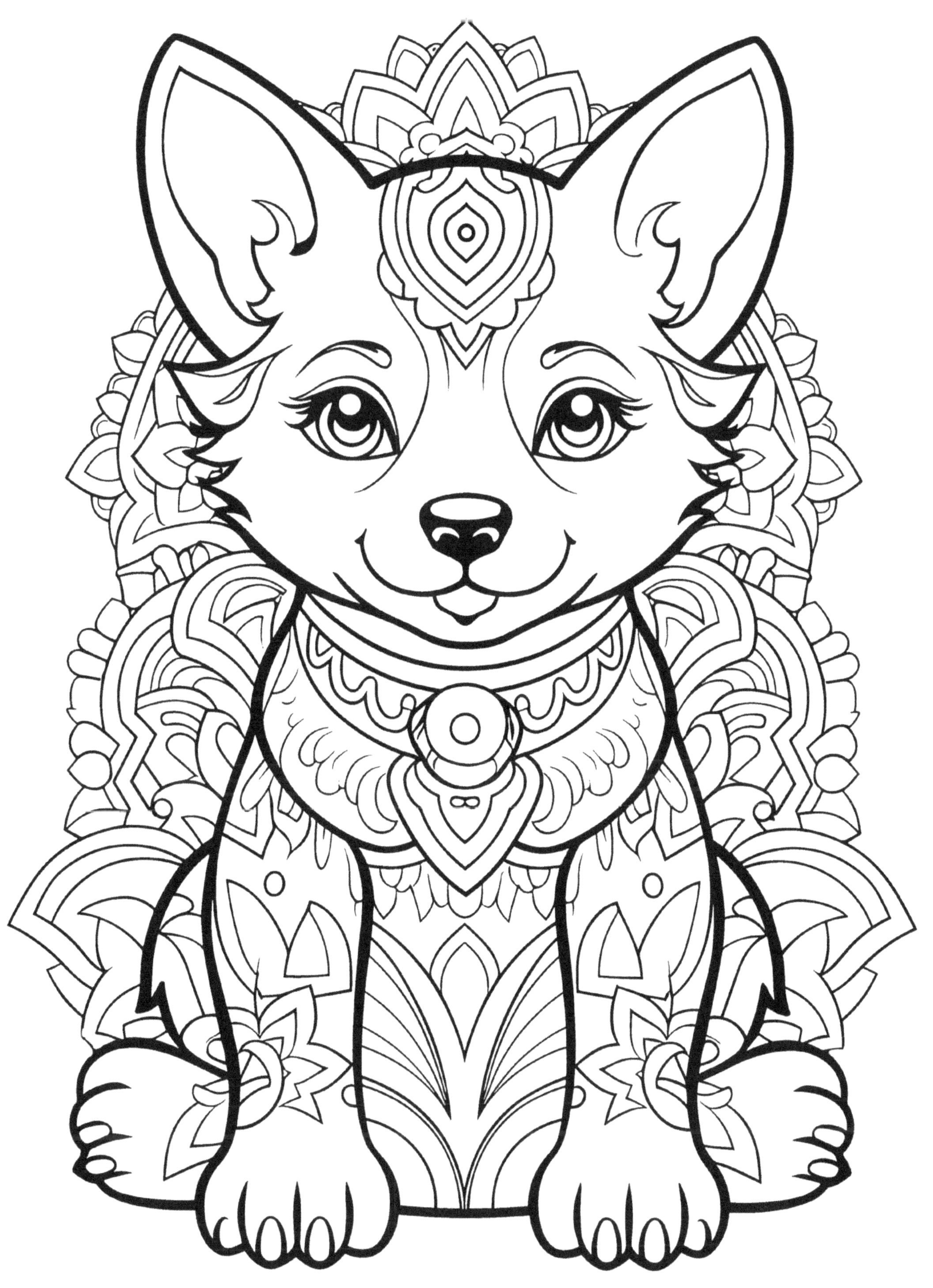

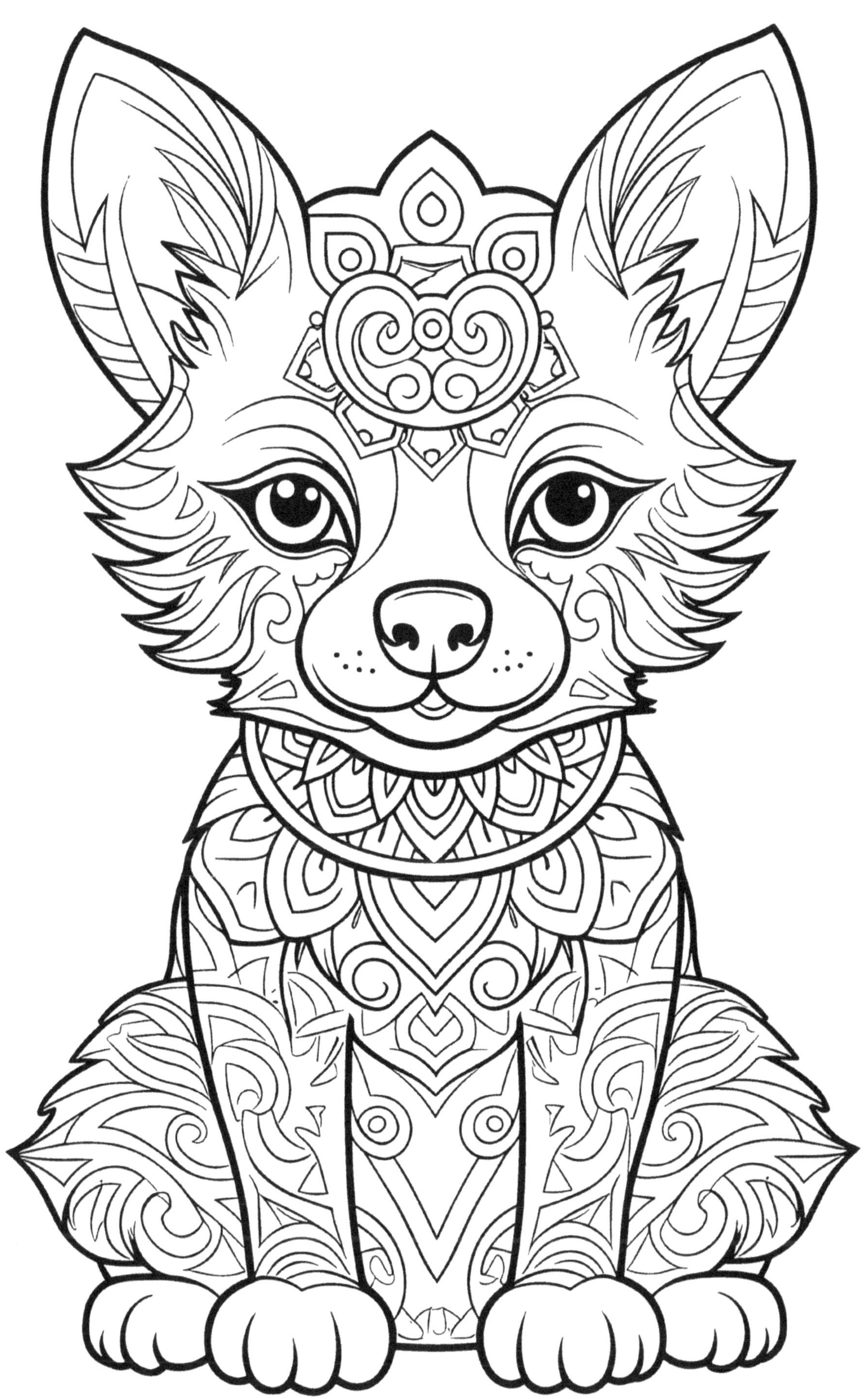

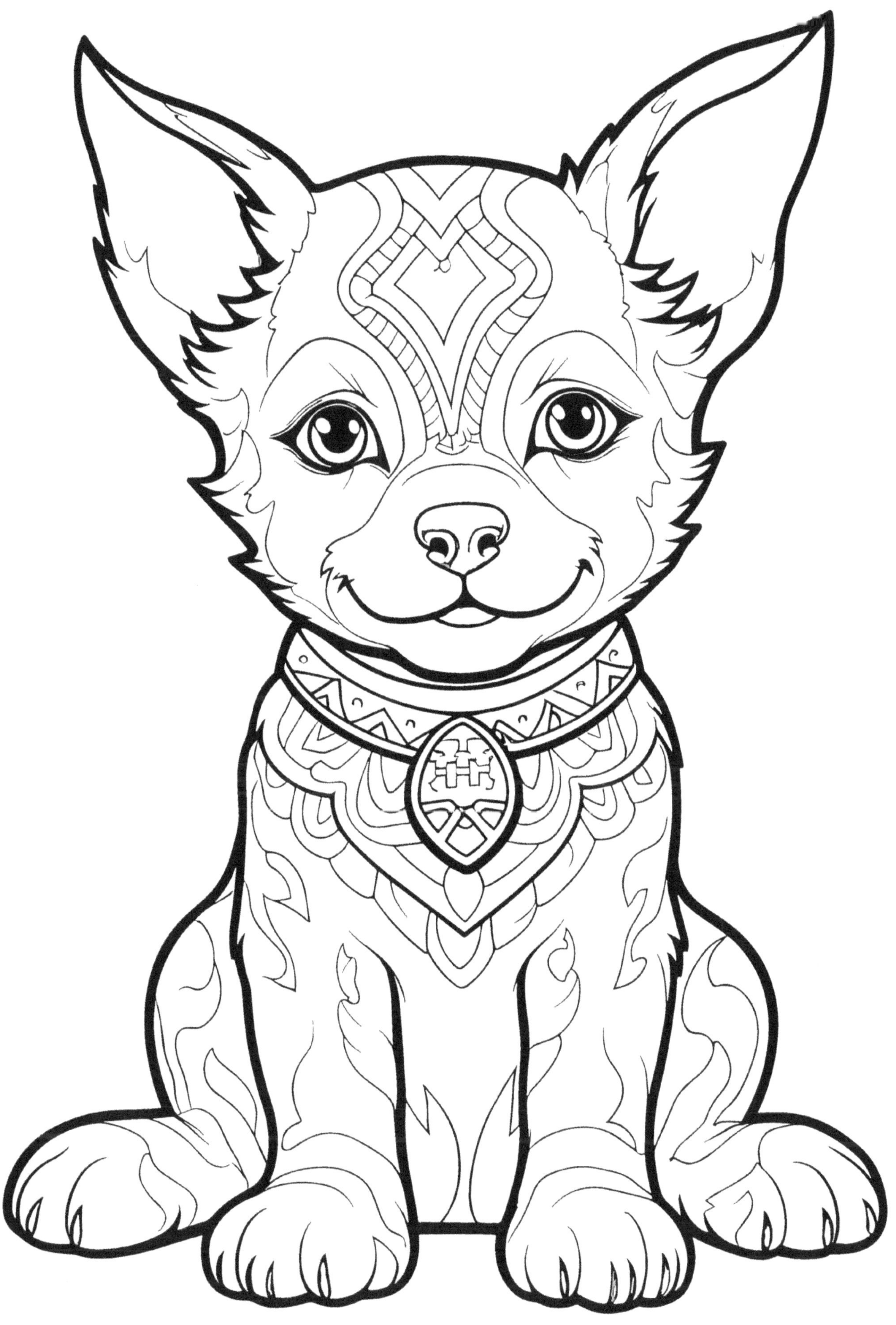

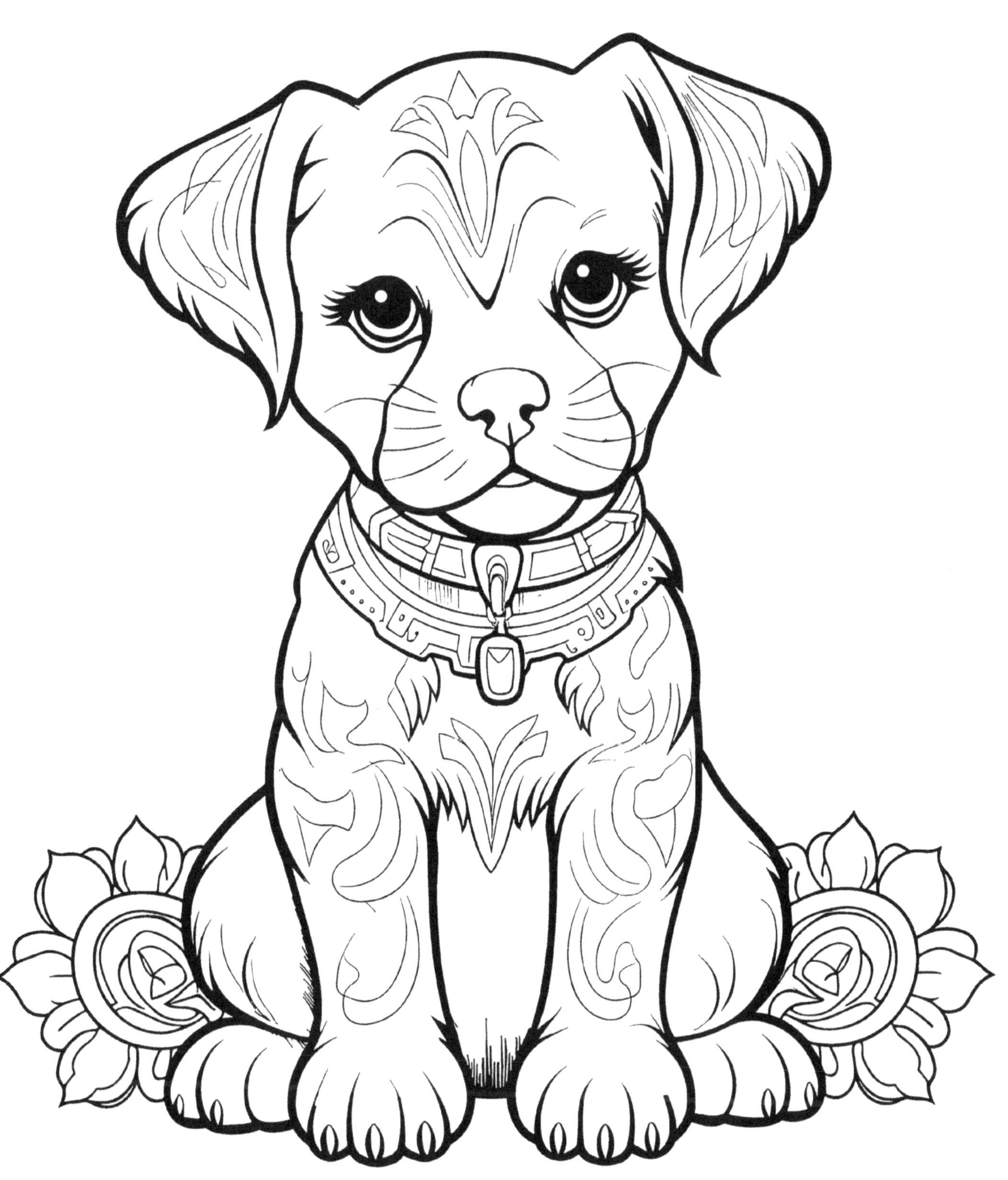

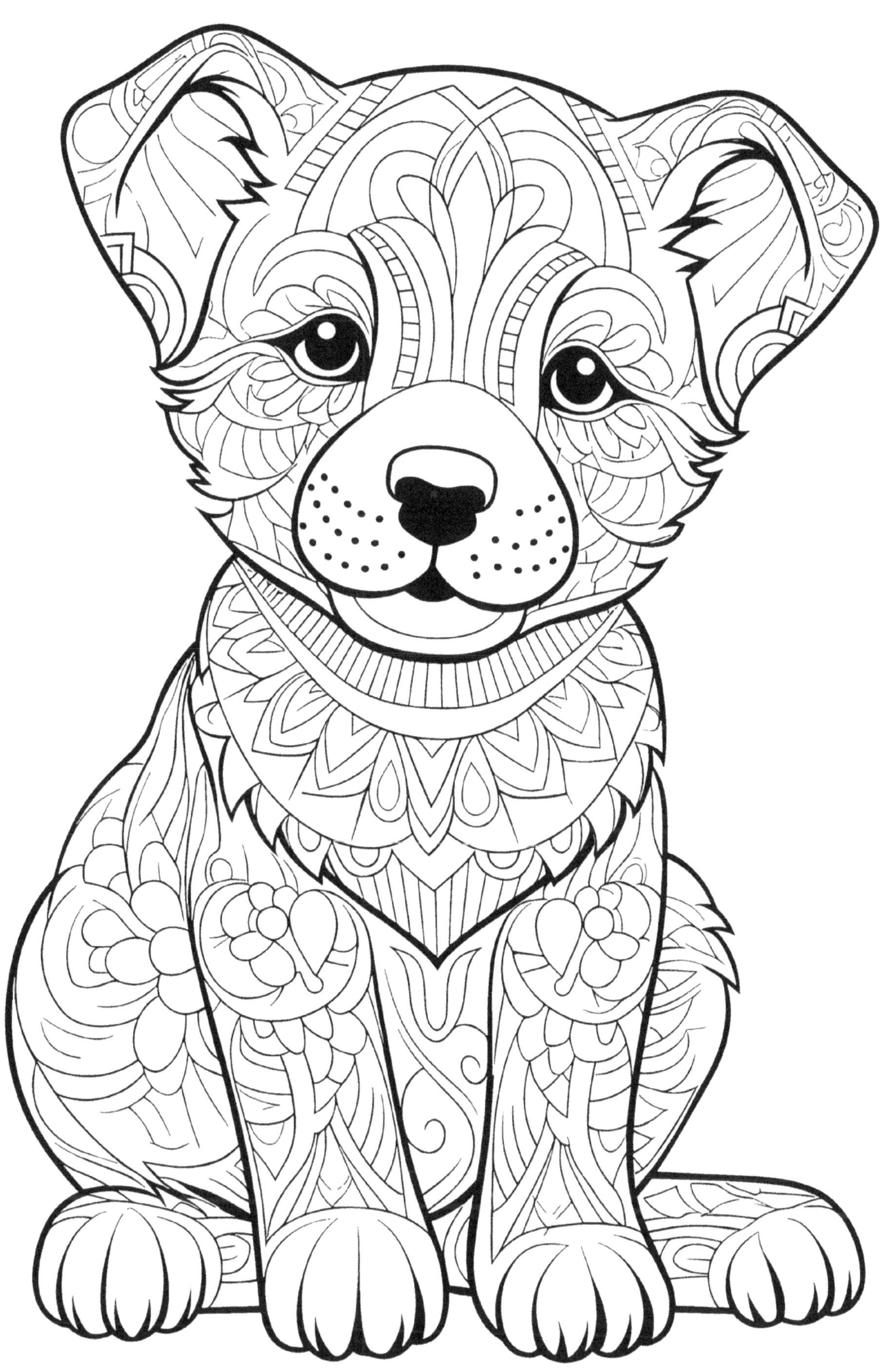

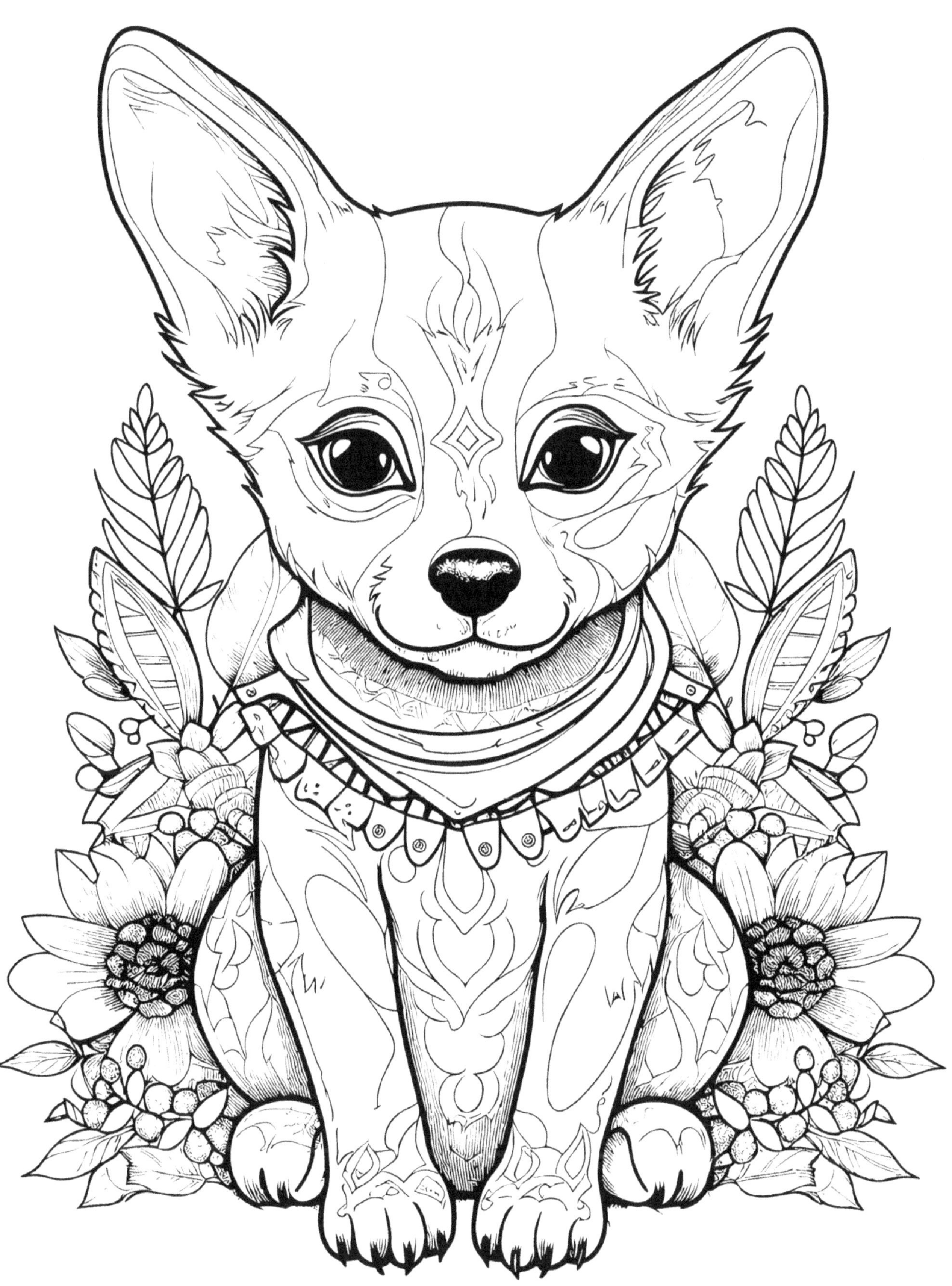

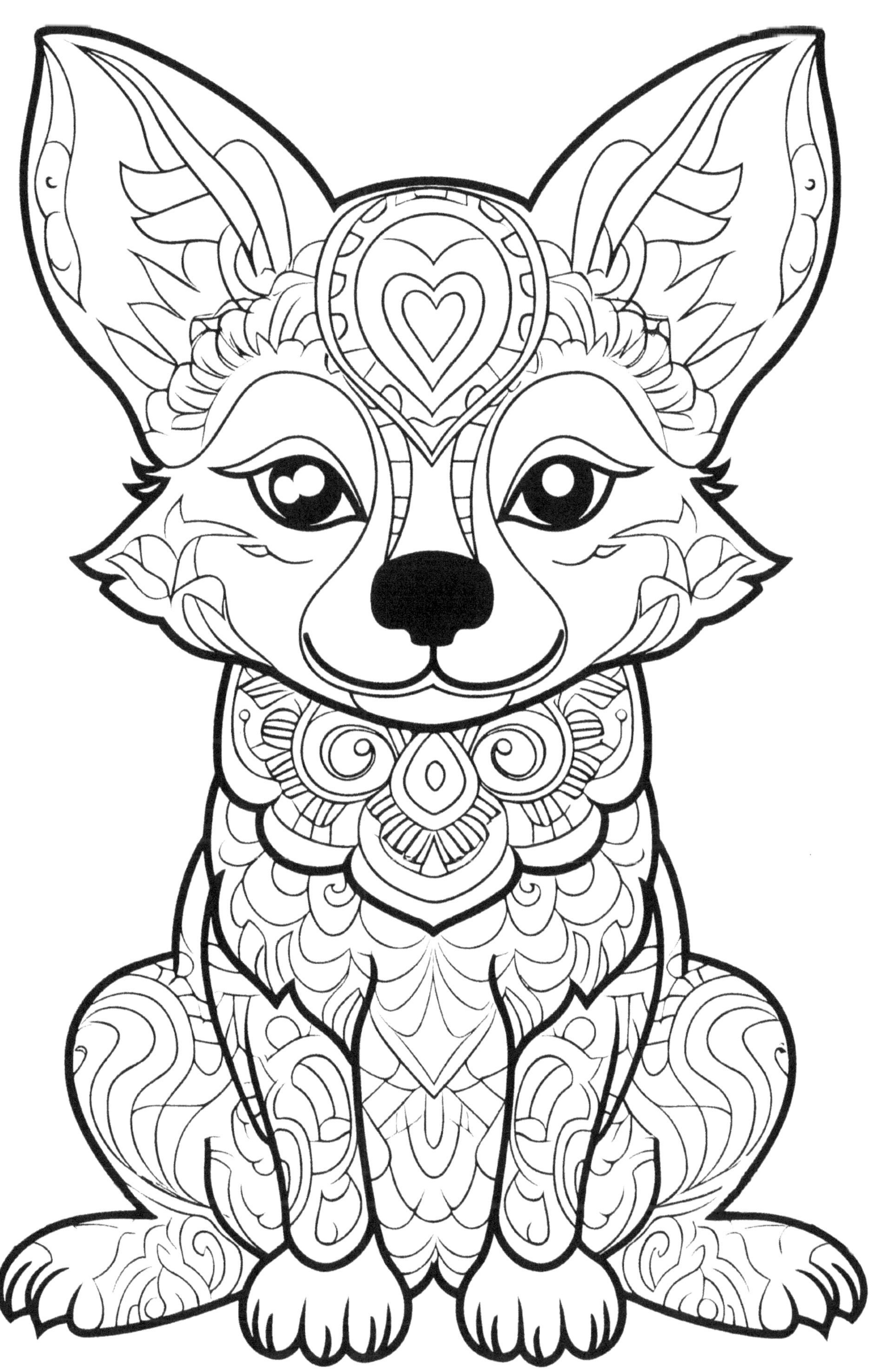

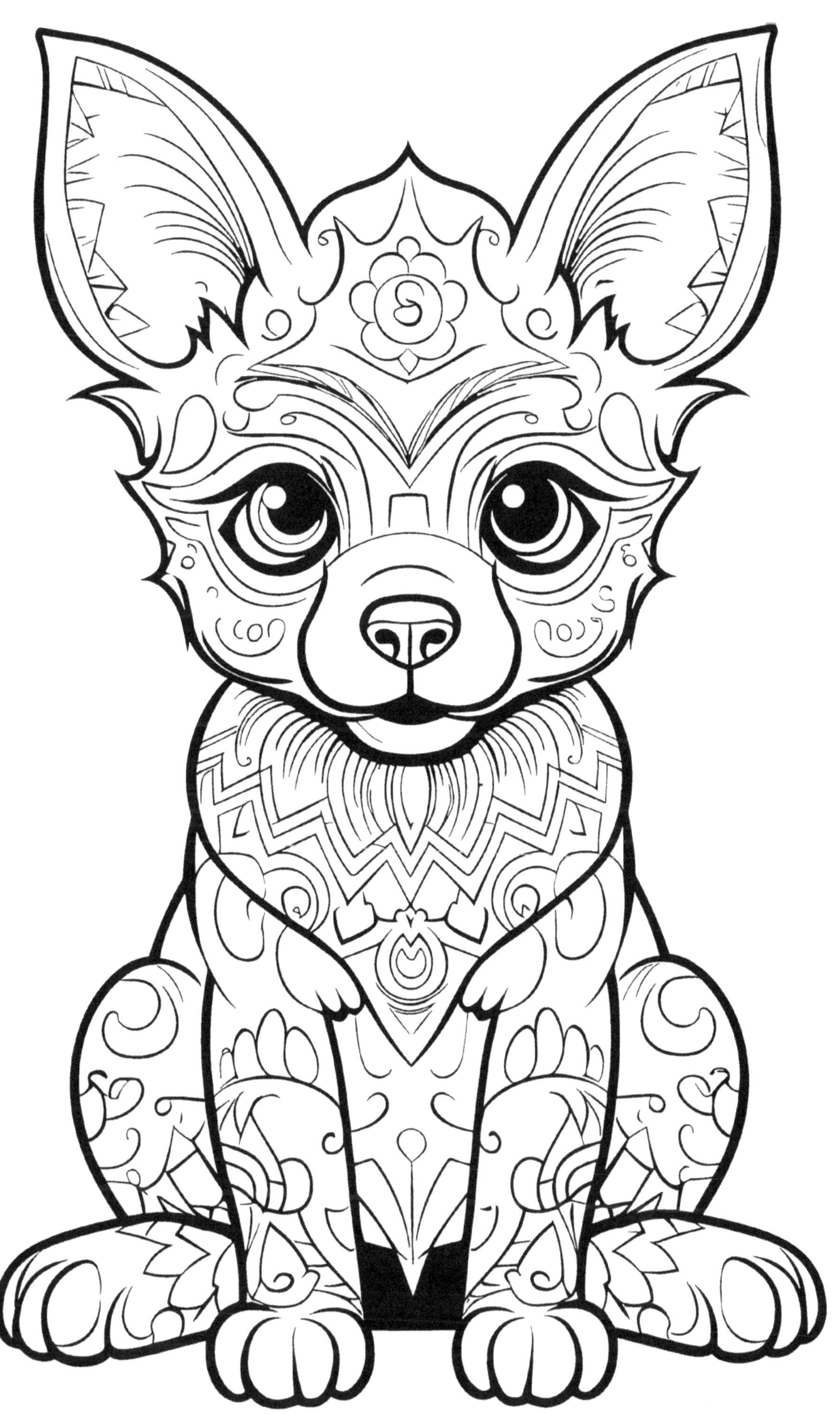

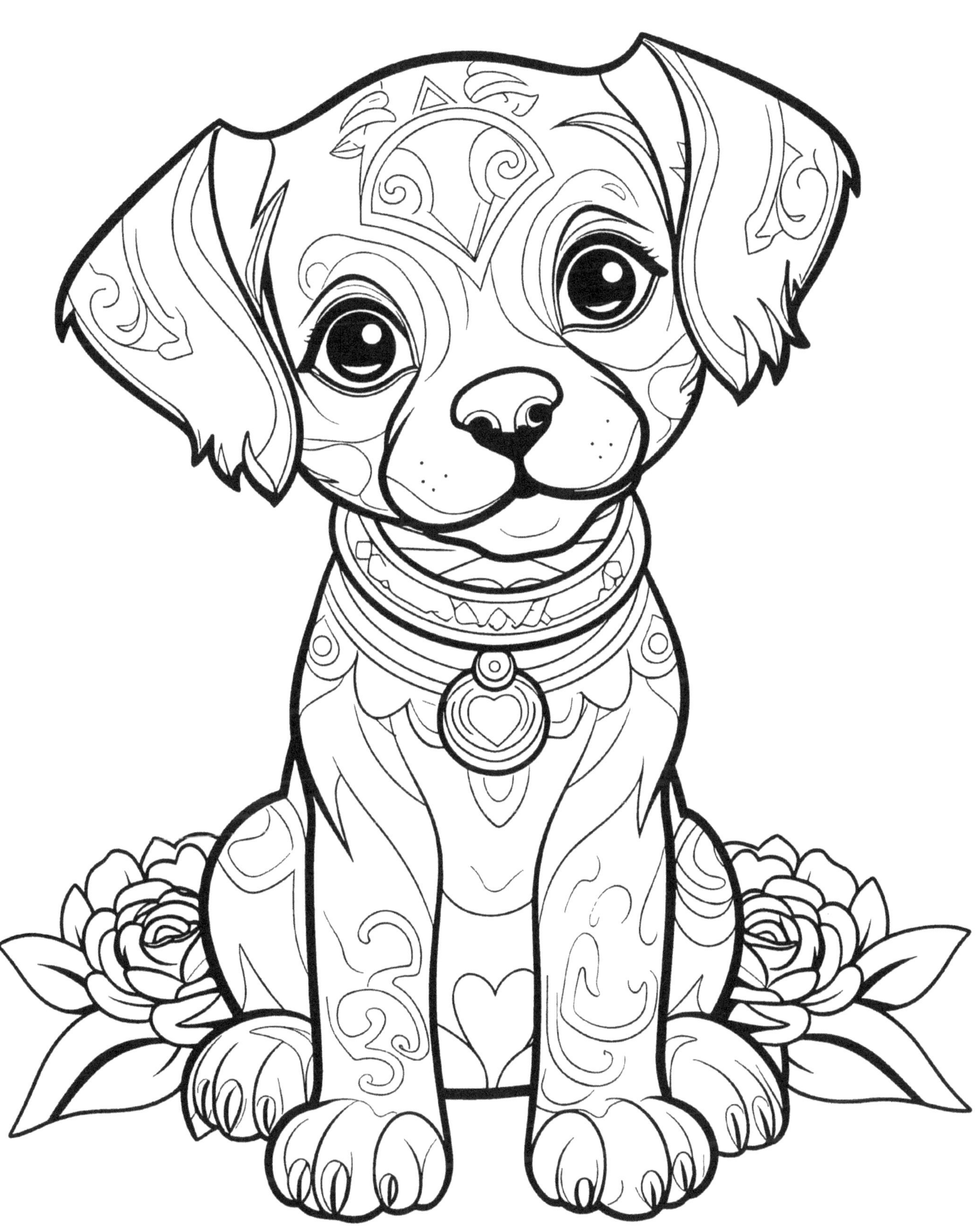

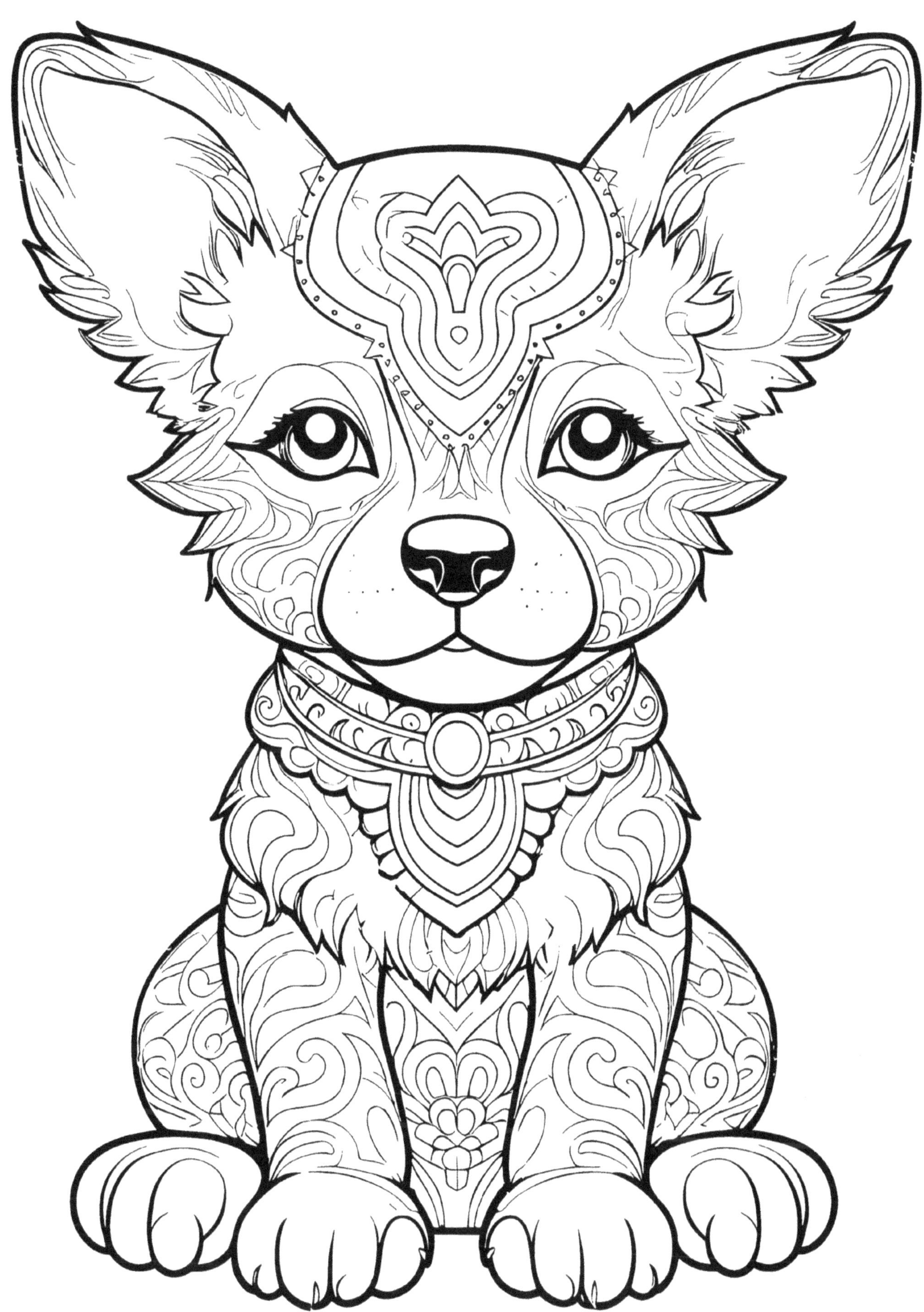

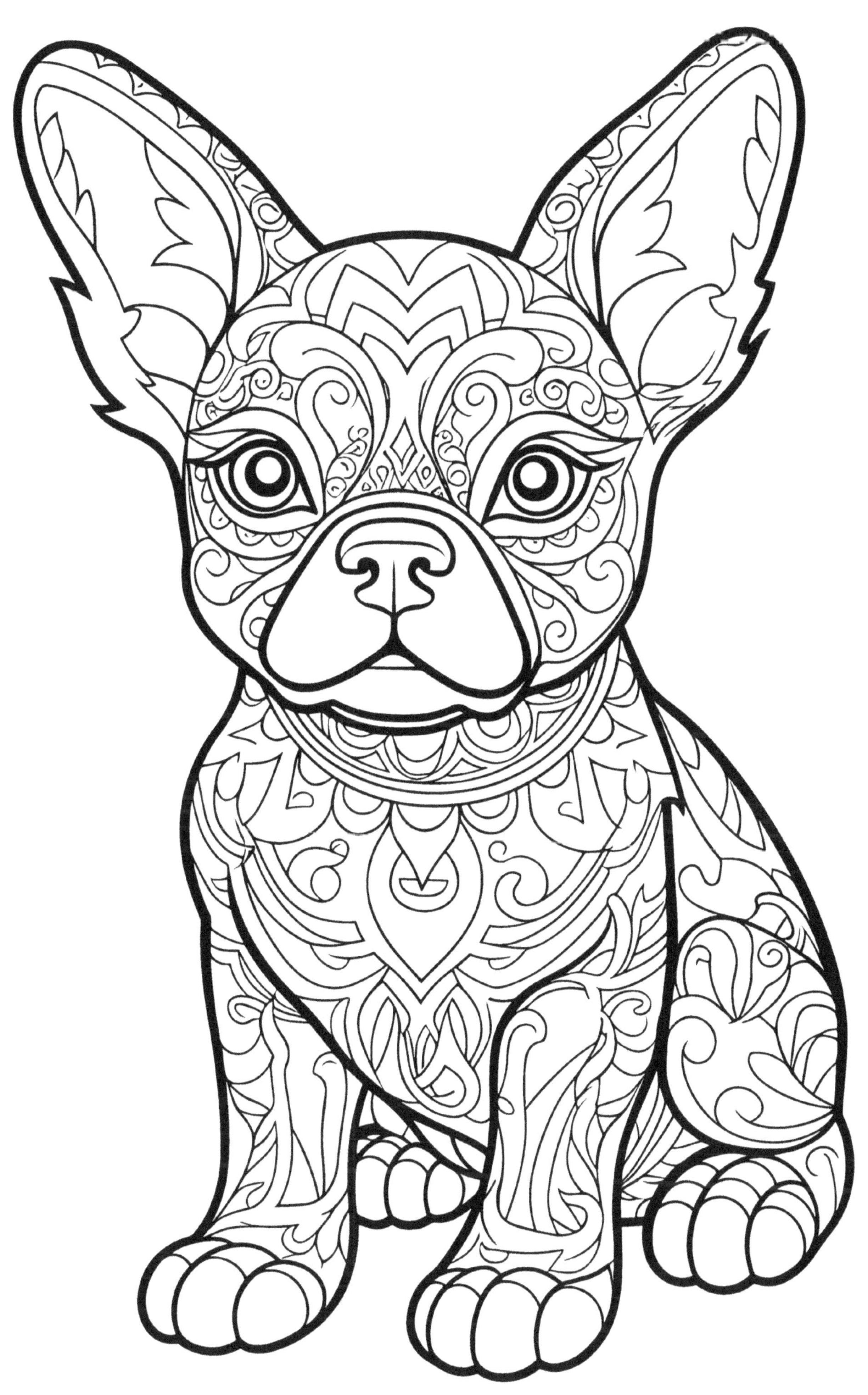

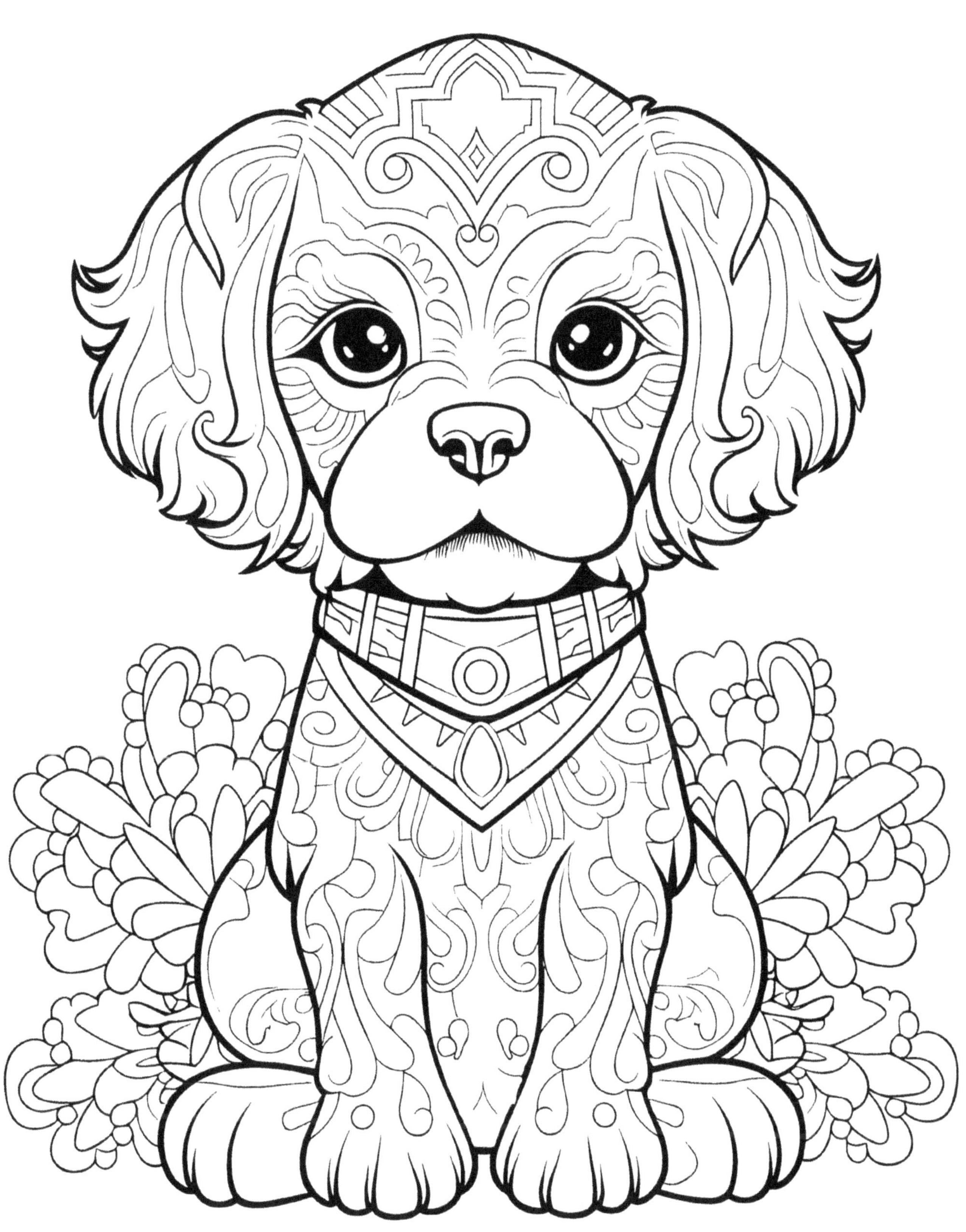

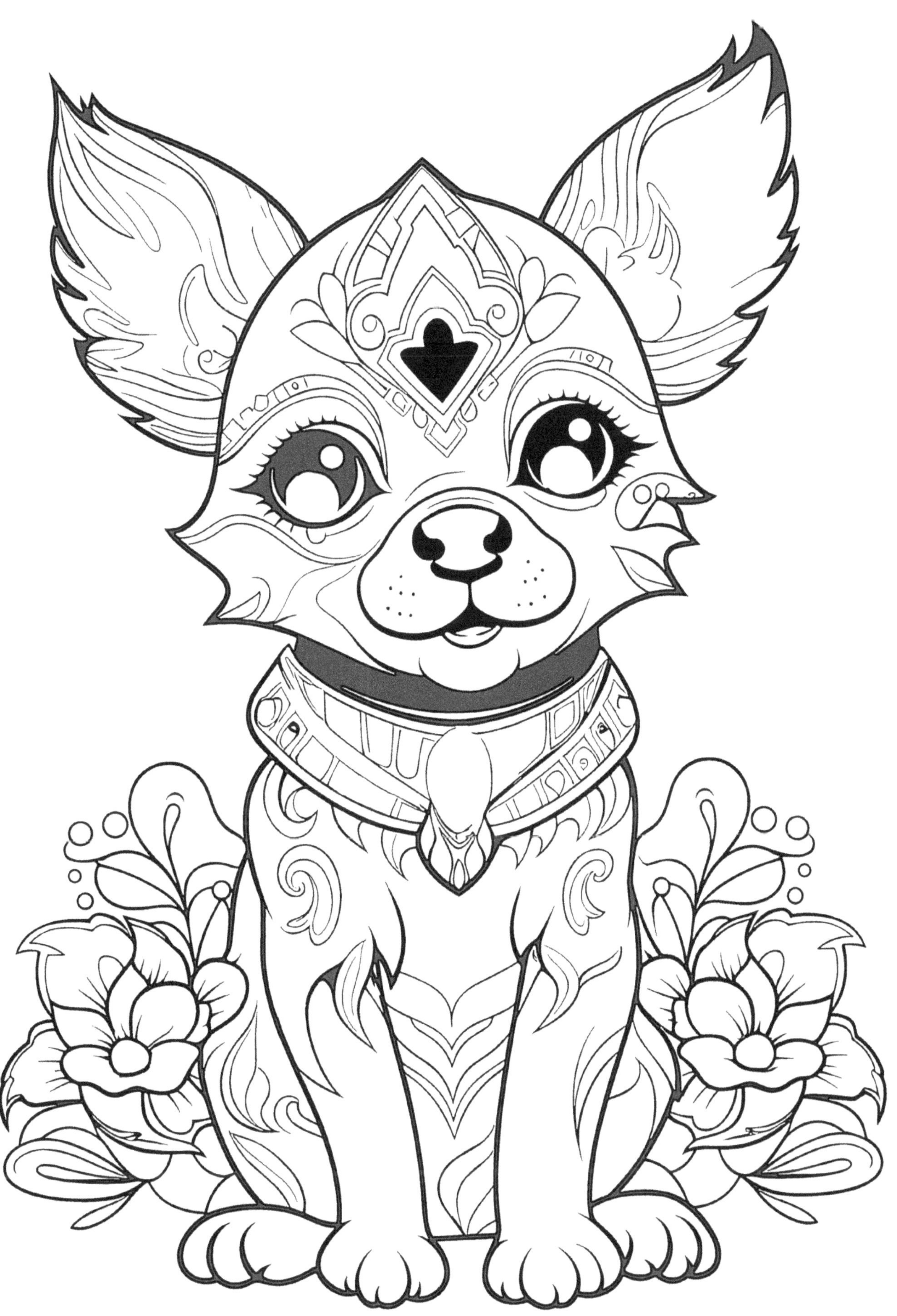

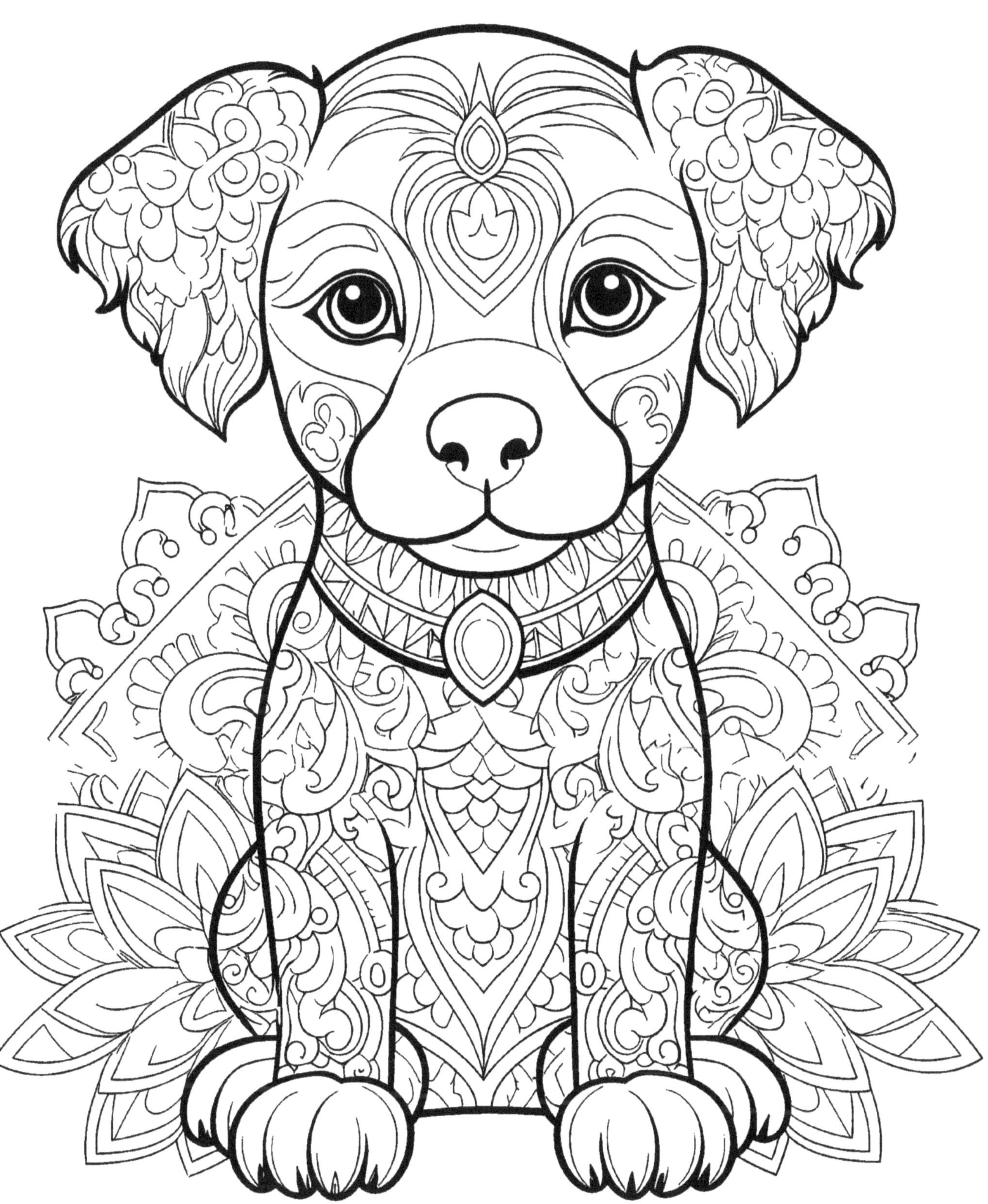

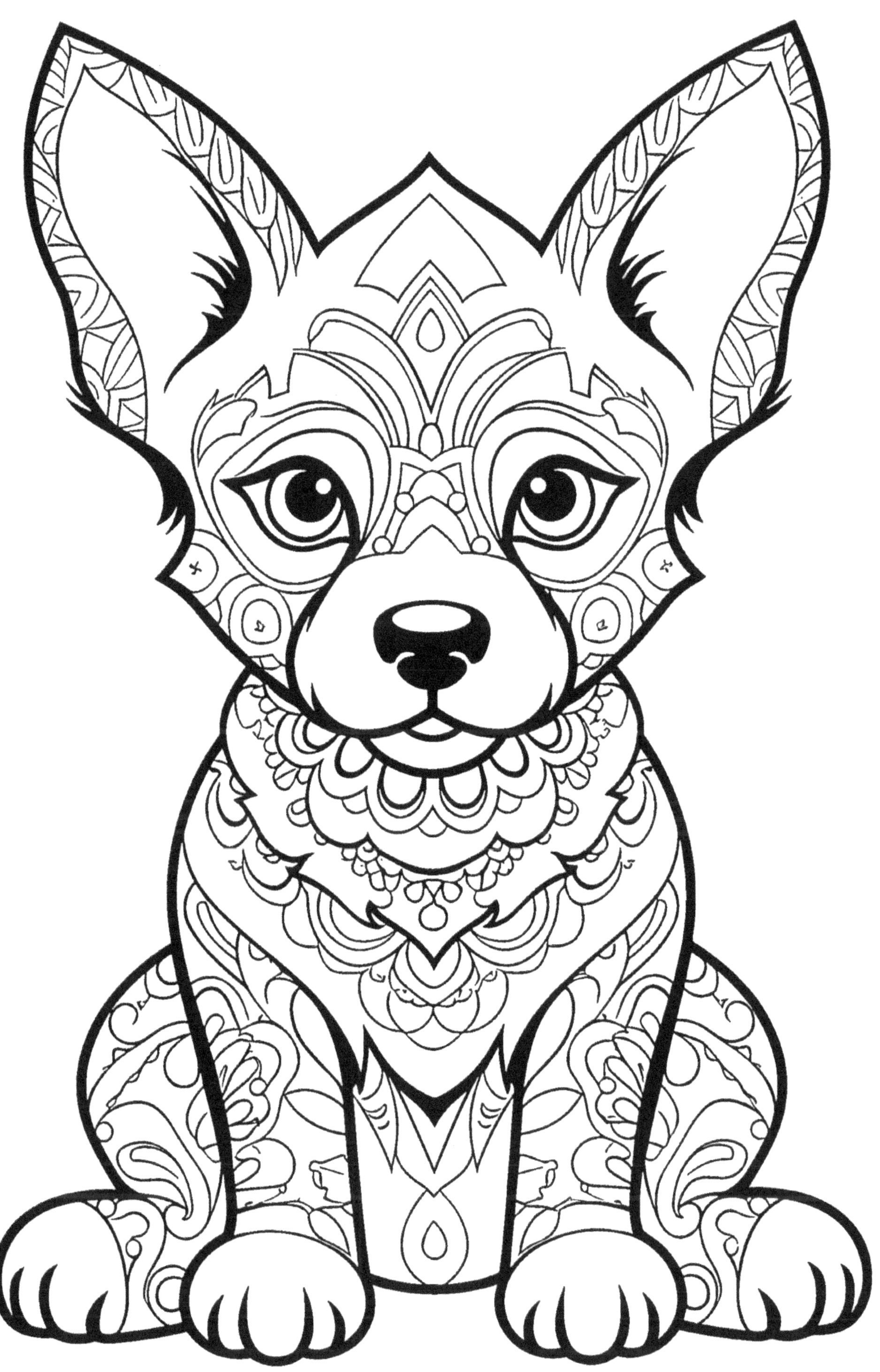

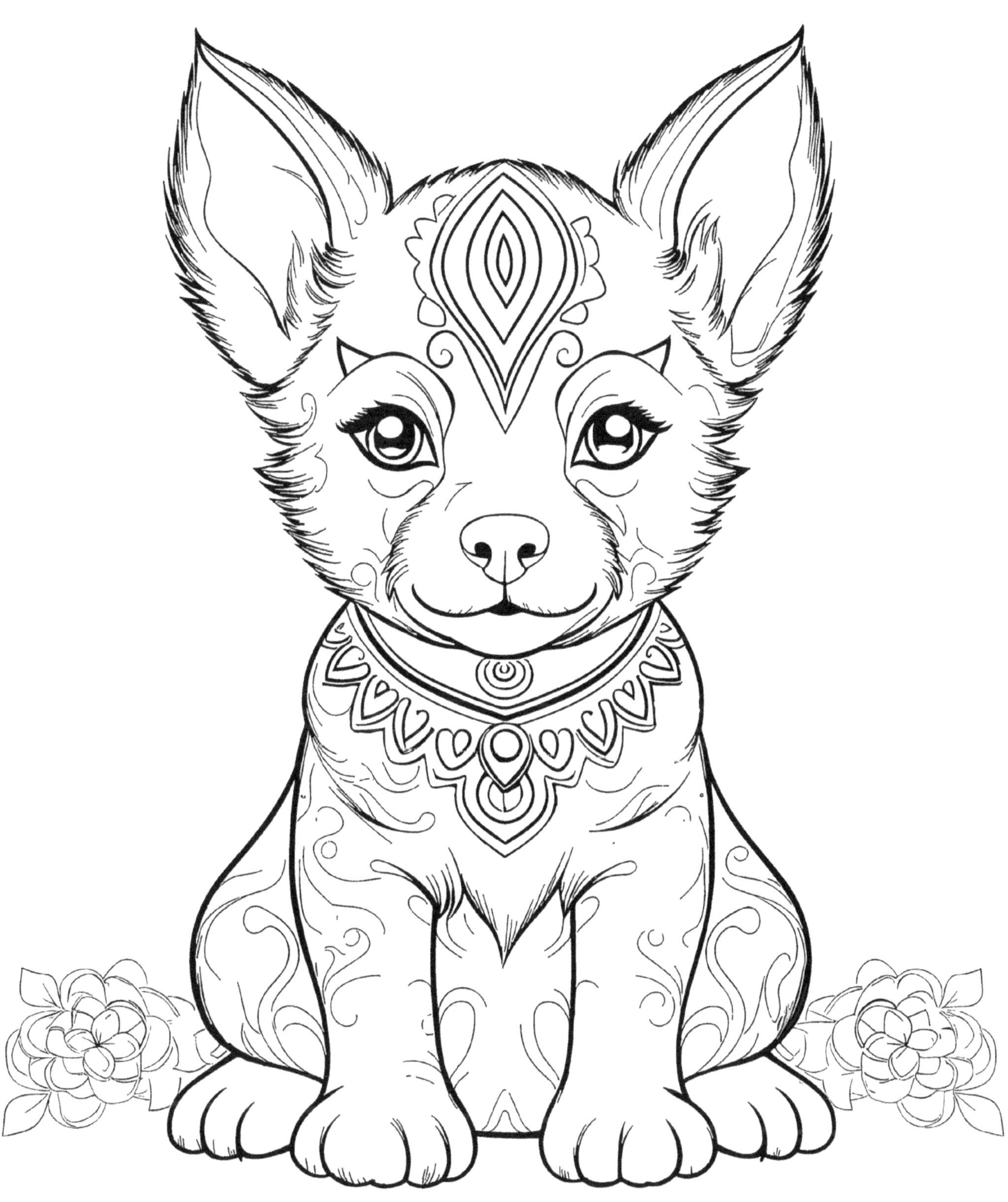

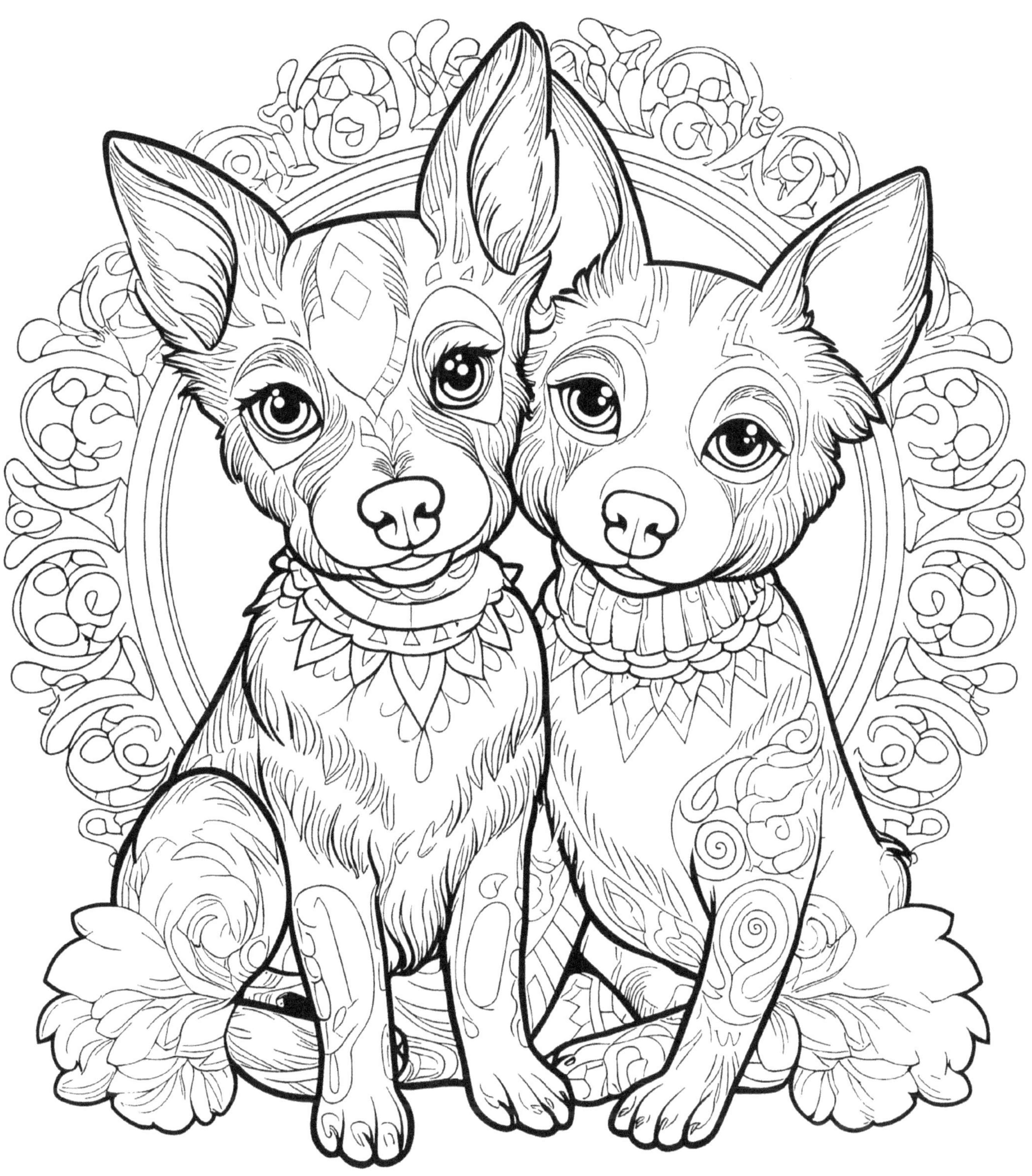